CYCLING ACROSS OREGON

STORIES, SURPRISES & REVELATIONS ALONG THE STATE'S SCENIC BIKEWAYS

DAN SHRYOCK

Cycling Across Oregon
Stories, Surprises & Revelations Along the State's Scenic Bikeways

For information about this book, contact the publisher:

Shryock Associates LLC
Salem, Oregon
www.danshryock.com
dan@danshryock.com

ISBN: 979-8-218-36589-9
Library of Congress Control Number: 2024903216

Printed in the United States of America

Editor: Bronte Dod
Design and Production: David Caplan / Feedback Graphics
Cover Photo: Dan Shryock

*To my family and friends who put in the miles
to make this all possible.*

Contents

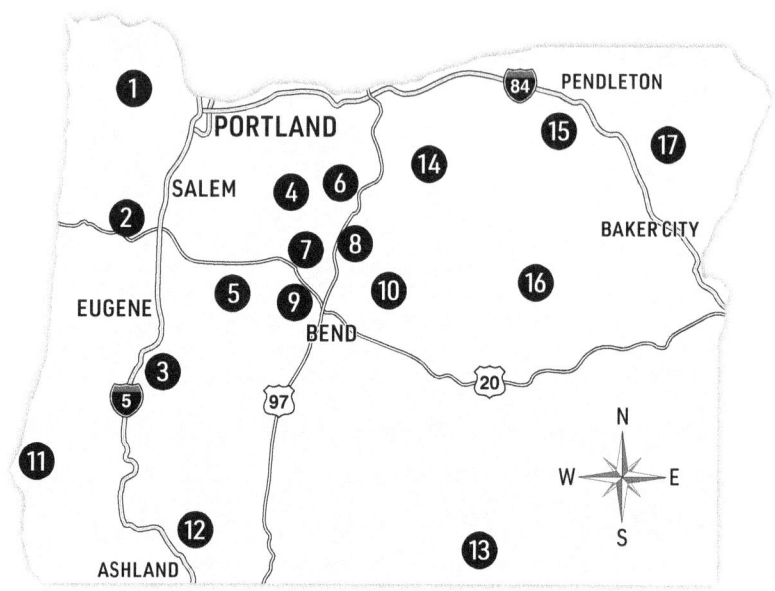

Scenic Bikeways Index

Prologue

I'm an Oregonian by choice. Our family's decision to move to the Willamette Valley was a career move with a bonus. We were fortunate to make this unique corner of the world our home and the Oregon Coast, the valley, and the Cascade Range quickly became our outdoor playground.

My perspective of the Oregon outdoors expanded once I started riding a bike. Exploring backroads between points on a map became as enjoyable as arriving at a destination. I wanted to see more, and that curiosity led to the decision to ride Oregon's 17 official scenic bikeways in 2021.

For some readers, these pages may be an introduction to the state bikeway system. But in a larger sense, this is a study of rural Oregon. What we found, what we experienced along the way left me in awe. And, while I wrote this book with cyclists in mind, I believe it can be a portal for anyone willing to slow down and fully see their surroundings. This is my narrative of discovery; I hope it energizes others to do the same.

This also is a collection of stories, a mix of history, geology, personalities, experiences, and revelations. Bikeways are described using a few cycling terms such as elevation gain, road grade percentage, and level of difficulty for those ready to ride. There are no turn-by-turn cue sheets, however; this is not a guidebook. Route maps and directions are available via the RidewithGPS. com website and app.

This tour was born from the COVID pandemic. Our small circle of cycling friends first began organizing weekend bike trips in 2019, but the virus forced us to alter our plans. Instead of traveling to different parts of the state, we put together day trips within a two-hour radius of Salem. We avoided traveling in the same car and met at a designated place each morning. We kept our space while riding and then circled socially distanced lawn chairs to relax and swap stories.

By January 2021, a COVID vaccine was available and optimism buoyed. I decided I wanted to ride all the bikeways in a single cycling season and a quick poll of the group—Bob Cortright, Patti Rogers, Eric Jacobson, and Jennifer Donnelly— made it unanimous.

But this would not be an endurance test. We wanted to acquaint ourselves with the remote reaches of Oregon, meet people in small towns as diverse as forested Vernonia in the northwest corner and arid Lakeview in the south-central high desert. It was about riding through John Day Fossil Beds National Monument for a look at Oregon's geologic past, witnessing the devastation of remote wildfires, and meeting owners of an eastern ghost town. It was about gaining a new perspective on Oregon's heritage by traveling on two wheels.

I first started road cycling in 2010 at Bob's encouragement. Knee pain signaled the end of my running-for-exercise days, and I needed a new outlet. Bob, a friend and neighbor, had long amused me with stories of his bike exploits on Italian vacations and he encouraged me to join him for local rides in Polk County. I finally accepted the offer.

And while I needed a new form of exercise, my motivation ran deeper. I watched the Tour de France on TV in 2008 a year after my first trip to Italy, my ancestral homeland. As I watched the professional peloton snake through Provence, I was captivated not by the cyclists or the competition but by the landscape, the medieval and Renaissance architecture, and the destinations. These hamlets with their stone construction reminded me of Tuscany. I was entranced day after day as TV broadcasters Phil Liggett and Paul Sherwen shared historical notes about each landmark as the racers zipped in long, single-file lines through narrow village streets. I was vicariously traveling through Europe by bike.

Cycling, I realized, creates the opportunity to see the countryside at slower speed, a chance to travel anytime I choose to get on a bike. My first ride with Bob and friend David Brooks was a 35-mile loop on local roads I'd driven many times at 55 mph. Now, at a fourth of that speed, I found myself examining what farmers were growing in their fields. I could scan the nearby hills and look across the valley as I passed wineries, a small 150-year-old church, and weathered, dilapidated barns.

Exercise and exploration. I was hooked.

More than a decade later, I've ridden in places I would have thought inconceivable years ago: Italy, England, New Zealand, Glacier National Park in Montana and Stanley Park in Vancouver, B.C., Whidbey Island in Washington state's Puget Sound and along the Southern California coast. But there's no place like riding at home in Oregon. I'm reminded of a ride Bob and I took several years ago after his return from a trip to Lucca, Italy. We were passing through the Eola Hills west of Salem when we crested a small rise and looked across vineyards and a valley below. "This is just as good as Italy," Bob said, taking me by surprise. "It's just as beautiful." He then paused and added, "but Italy has the food."

Agreed. Italian cuisine is worth the trip, but I can ride from my own home into the Oregon countryside anytime I wish.

We rode a total of 24 days and about 1,500 miles during our scenic bikeways expedition. Bob, Eric, and Patti were along for many of the rides. Others, including my wife Carla and son Sam, joined some days as well.

Along the way, I realized how unique each locale could be and I began stopping to simply appreciate the hills, the rivers, and the open land. It's now a ritual each time I ride my bike. I stop and ask myself if I would ever have had the opportunity to be in this place had I not ridden a bicycle? Bikes are the vehicles that can take us to new places, new people, and new experiences. The scenic bikeways are the directional arrows pointing to revelations around the next bend. This is why I ride.

It wasn't possible to stop and engage people in lengthy conversations along the road. We had miles to cover and a schedule to keep. Chats typically ended with me gathering names, email addresses, phone numbers, and perhaps business cards and that led to longer, meaningful conversations weeks later. Each follow-up interview reminded me of a moment on the road and often helped put an experience in better perspective.

Perhaps the most moving revelation came from Bobbie Conner, director of the Tamástslikt Cultural Institute on the Umatilla Indian Reservation in Eastern Oregon, as we discussed the cycling experience across the land of her ancestors.

"My grandmother traveled [these roads] on horseback as a child with her family. They didn't know them by a forestry road number," she told me. "They knew them intimately, and I think cyclists have a chance to experience the intimacy with a loved landscape. It has been loved for millennia, it has been cherished for millennia. It's a route passing through not just one precious place but a series of precious places. They are all strung together there.

"It's a sense of mindfulness and conscientious traveling."

Like Bobbie's ancestors, we traveled at a slower speed. We saw the land and traversed its undulations. We heard the waters, smelled the fields, felt the breeze, and studied the sky. Our understanding of and appreciation for the land grew with each pedal stroke.

We were mindful of our sense of place.

1

The Best Places to Ride

It's 45 degrees outside and this January wind presses against my face as I pedal up a quiet backroad high in the West Salem hills. I'm dressed in layers for the cold and a balaclava warms my head as I look east to the western slopes of the Cascade Range. Mount Hood with its bright white snowcap shimmers to my left against a pale blue sky. Mount Jefferson is visible; so is Mount Washington.

This is my first ride of the year and I'm excited to be getting in shape despite the cold. I need to be in good riding form to keep up with the others.

This is a diverse group. Bob Cortright is our alpha rider with a competitive spirit; a description Bob considers generous. He rides his bike most every day, often ignoring Oregon's winter rain, wind, and the rare Willamette Valley snowfall. He seeks out the challenge—hill hunting, he calls it—and often detours from our day's plan whenever he sees a side road tilting up. We don't follow; he will do his thing and then catch up. When he sees another rider, a stranger, ahead on any road, he looks to us with his I'm-going-to-catch-him grin and then rises from his bike saddle, stomps on the pedals, and accelerates toward his prey.

Eric Jacobson and Jennifer Donnelly enjoy climbing as well and can keep pace with Bob most of the time. Both Eric and Jennifer are consistent, steady riders. I've seen Jennifer push the pace one day and slide back to ride alongside slower people the next. Both embrace the socializing that cycling provides us. Jennifer sometimes plots what she calls "hills of pain" to tempt Bob. She'll lead us all to the bottom of a road known only to her and then encourages Bob to go for it. Eric sometimes takes the bait as well.

Patti Rogers and I, on the other hand, avoid anything labeled "pain." Patti is my bike peer. We usually ride together no matter the pace. When we climb, we fall behind the others. Patti zigzags up quiet country inclines to take the sting out of a steep grade much like a sailboat tacking against the wind. I slowly move straight ahead. We usually finish each hill at the same time.

I try not to be the lanterne rouge, the last rider to arrive at the top. It's a term that originated in the early years of the Tour de France. The last rider to complete the 21-day bike race was called the lanterne rouge, the red lantern, the light on the back of a train. I often claim the honor; everyone else knows they will have time to rest once they crest. I embrace my perseverance. I may be the slowest, but I make it to the top without walking every time.

And, after all, it doesn't matter who is fastest up or down a hill, who is first and who is last. These are my riding partners, my friends. This is our group and we're ready to take on these backroads together.

I push on alone today despite the cold. The irony is not lost; I'm the one least likely to venture out when temperatures drop below 50 degrees. I don't like the cold and shiver at the thought of pedaling in this weather. Today is different. I want to get started.

The official statement from the state Parks and Recreation Department reads: "The mission of the Oregon Scenic Bikeways Program is to establish a thriving, lasting collection of the best places to ride a bicycle in Oregon."

The best places to ride a bicycle in Oregon.

That's open for debate. For some cyclists, a lap around the rim of Crater Lake in Southern Oregon is one of the best rides in the state. Imagine pedaling in a national park, looking across an expanse of deep water so clear, so blue, so bright it nearly hurts your eyes. A ring of rocky peaks, some still snow-capped in summer, provides a backdrop. Wizard Island, a cinder cone reminder of past volcanic eruptions, juts from the water. The Phantom Ship, an eroded rock formation reminiscent of a pirate ship, appears to sail across the surface. The thin air—the lake is 6,173 feet above sea level and the roadway is higher than that—fatigues the less-conditioned cyclist.

But, there are too many tourists driving cars and RVs on the park's sometimes winding two-lane Rim Drive, some say. It's simply too dangerous.

A less experienced, less confident bike rider, meanwhile, could conclude the best place to ride is on a vehicle-free network of paved trails like those found in Salem's Minto-Brown Island Park. This wooded floodplain is very safe, they could argue.

Neither of these routes are state scenic bikeways, yet both can be considered worthy destinations. Minto-Brown was never proposed for the program. Crater Lake was submitted by local proponents but rejected by the state, in part, because of scheduled road repairs within the national park each year that would pose problems for motorists and cyclists alike.

Bikeways that meet the requirements and have been accepted in the program provide variety for anyone who wants to ride. Rated by difficulty, these routes—one easy, eight moderate, three challenging, five extreme—are representative of the best, diverse places to ride in Oregon.

The original idea for a scenic bikeway started in 2008 with Cycle Oregon, a nonprofit group that has been staging weeklong events in different regions of the state for more than 30 years. Organizers thought a designated state route should be mapped through the Willamette Valley. Working with the Oregon State Parks, they created a 134-mile course from Champoeg State Heritage Area south to the town of Coburg. The first scenic bikeway was born.

Sensing a larger opportunity, cycling advocates successfully convinced the state legislature in 2009 to create a scenic bikeways program, the first of its kind in the nation with defined goals of promoting the state's natural beauty and cultural heritage while stimulating economic development in rural communities.

It seems to be working. A 2021 study by Earth Economics, commissioned by Oregon state agencies, indicated road cycling statewide generates nearly $1.29 billion in spending a year when calculating to include bike tourists. Road cyclists combine to ride about 10.8 million days a year and spend $119 each day on average. And with the scenic bikeways located across Oregon, almost every region of the state is enjoying some benefit.

But who would want to ride a bike in the rain? Despite the myth, it does not rain here 12 months a year. Sure, winters force us to describe precipitation in a variety of ways, if only to avoid redundancy—mist, drizzle, sprinkles, showers, rain, and steady rain. By May, however, there's a reasonable chance days will be dry. From June to October, expect the best weather imaginable. Humidity seemingly is non-existent.

Here's another misconception: Oregon is blanketed with forests from border to border. The official state tree is the dominant Douglas fir, but much of this terrain is farms, high desert, or remote grazing land. Think sagebrush and amber waves of wheat. To better understand the state's geography, look at a map and visualize vertical sections from west to east. Start at the Pacific coast with beaches, oceanside towns, and Highway 101. Now move east and find the Coast Range with its highest point, Marys Peak near Corvallis, topping at 4,101 feet.

East of the Coast Range is the Willamette Valley, a fertile farming region and the center of Oregon's population base. The Willamette Valley extends from Portland and the Columbia River south past Salem, Corvallis, Albany, and Eugene, ending near Cottage Grove. Interstate 5 runs through the valley and continues south toward California, passing through the Umpqua and Rogue valleys. The famous Rogue River and the lesser-known Umpqua River are found here; cities include Roseburg, Grants Pass, Medford, and Ashland.

Move east to the Cascade Range, a string of mountains stretching from British Columbia to California. The volcanic Cascades have been erupting for millions of years. Perhaps the most famous blast in Oregon was the eruption of Mount Mazama more than 7,700 years ago. That blast forced the mountain to collapse on itself and create a caldera, the volcanic crater we now call Crater Lake, Oregon's only national park. The most recent, significant volcanic eruption in the Cascades was Mount St. Helens in southern Washington. That 1980 explosion killed 57 people and caused widespread destruction. Mount Hood, Oregon's highest peak and our most famous mountain, is an active volcano, according to the U.S. Geological Survey. The peak, visible from downtown Portland, is not expected to blow again anytime soon.

Lands east of the Cascades are high, arid desert or open ranchland. More mountains—the Ochoco, Wallowa, and Blue mountains—rise in the northeast quadrant of the state. Whether it was the geography, climate, transportation, or industry, this region never gained a population foothold like regions west of the Cascades. For perspective, Eastern Oregon's boundaries cover two thirds of the state and hold just 4 percent of the state's population—not that anyone who lives there is complaining. What it lacks in population it makes up for in diverse terrain, miles of solitude, and some of the darkest skies in the country.

But what qualifies a bike route to be labeled an official scenic bikeway? I asked Alexandra Phillips, the longtime scenic bikeways coordinator for Oregon State Parks, to explain. Alex, as her friends call her, spent 10 years on the job before moving to Colorado. She and other members of the state's Active Bikeways Advisory Committee rode each mile of each proposed route, evaluated conditions based on natural qualities, "human-made" qualities such as buildings, heritage sites, and points of interest, and finally sensory qualities such as pleasant sounds and aromas. They also considered road safety.

"Once something is designated as an Oregon scenic bikeway, it's different than any other ride," Alex says. "Riders are expecting the best of the best. They're expecting it to be fully vetted."

I'm reminded of riding last year through Gibson Canyon east of Lakeview along the Oregon Outback Scenic Bikeway. Alone on the road, I could hear rushing water, yet I saw nothing but rock, dirt, and scrub brush. Eventually the aptly named Deep Creek, which was cut low into the rock on the south side of Highway 140, came into view and eventually ran nearly level with the road. A few more pedal strokes and Deep Creek Falls appeared, water tumbling 25 feet on its easterly flow. Natural and sensory qualities.

Alex explains the designation process. Local government entities and cycling advocates team to propose a route. These proponents gather local support and secure commitments from their city and county road departments to maintain the routes. Once the advisory committee test rides and recommends a proposed route, state officials make the final decision. Only then are directional scenic bikeway signs installed. Thirty-five routes have been proposed by 2021 but only 17 made the cut.

So, I ask Alex, which scenic bikeway is your favorite? Where would you ride on your next visit back in Oregon?

"I love anything east of the Cascades," she says without hesitation. "We have some of those super-green bikeways on the west side, but I love the Grande Tour [near Baker City]. I've probably ridden the Grande Tour more than any of them. I love the Blue Mountain Century and I've ridden the Old West quite a bit. I just love the east side, any of them."

She recalls debates with Natalie Inouye, a destination marketing vice president with Travel Lane County in Eugene and a member of the advisory committee. "I don't love riding with lots of trees. That's where I disagree with Natalie. We would have these constant arguments. She's like, 'it's so green. It's so beautiful. This is the best bikeway.' And I'm like, 'it's too green. There are too many trees. I can't see anything.'"

I quickly contact Natalie.

"Oh yes, we are east-west divided," Natalie confirms. "We've had a lot of fun with that. I tend to like a little more green, a little more water. I like the routes that are high on the natural qualities and have those sensory experiences. Sensory for me is deep in the woods and sensory for Alex is wide in the desert."

Few scenic bikeways offer both forests and deserts, Natalie points out. "You have to pick which side of the mountains you want to be on. Do you want the forests or the desert?"

I ask Alex why other beautiful routes don't make the cut. Crater Lake was rejected. The Historic Columbia River Highway, a marquee destination along the Columbia Gorge, was incomplete at the time of application. Approval would have placed bicyclists on the shoulder of Interstate 84. That wasn't going to happen.

Then there's Highway 101 along the Oregon Coast, a popular drive from Washington state and California. Much of the highway is a winding, sometimes narrow two-lane road. "The Oregon Coast wasn't a good idea," Alex says, "because . . . "

"Because you could die," I interrupt.

"Exactly. We call it the pucker factor."

"What's the pucker factor?"

"We actually came up with something called the pucker factor," she explains when pressed for a definition. "Um, it's when you're just so tense that you're puckering up some muscles that you use for other things that you normally don't tighten when you're biking."

Countless cyclists ride that highway every year despite the risks. They either have a low fear threshold or do a lot of puckering. Still, there are areas along Highway 101 that are pucker-free. I won't hesitate to ride along the South Coast where the road shoulder, or paved safety berm, is wide and safe.

But road shoulders are not a constant throughout the state. Most of the program's 1,260 miles are on low-volume, rural roads that don't see heavy traffic and don't even have shoulders.

Natalie describes herself as a confident rider—provided she is in her own comfort zone. She credits the scenic bikeways program for providing a sense of security. "I tend to like the routes that are more rural, and I definitely need the ones providing that comfort level. What I like about the bikeways program is that I know somebody else has already evaluated that. I know it's safe."

Someone once told me bicycling should be fun. It should be enjoyment rather than work. Therefore, the term training should not be used when describing preparation for an upcoming tour. That means I'm riding my bike up West Salem's hills in winter cold for pleasure. I must relish feeling my body chill as the bike speeds back down the same pavement I just climbed.

We'll start on our 2021 journey in a few weeks. It's time to remind both lungs and legs how much fun we're about to have searching for our comfort zone.

WILD RIVERS COAST SCENIC BIKEWAY

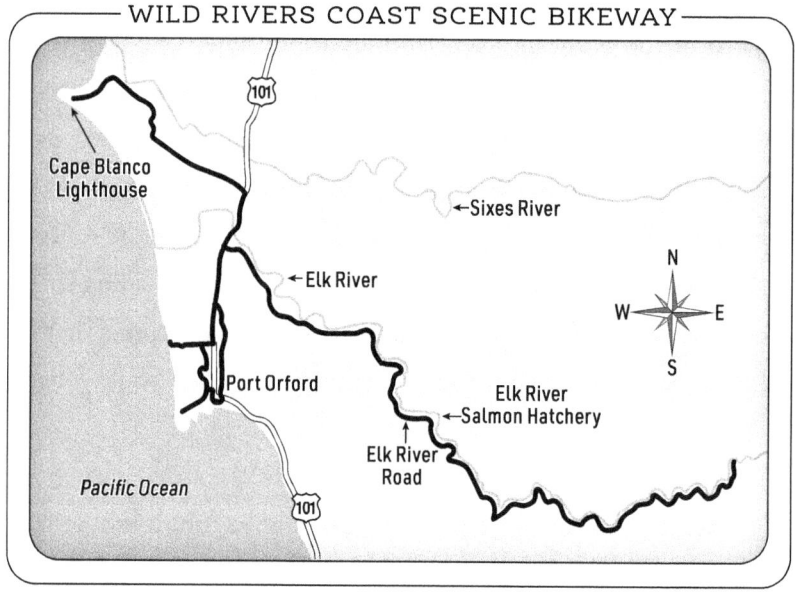

2

'The Formula Works'
Wild Rivers Coast Scenic Bikeway

• • •

Start and Finish: Port Orford
Distance: 61 miles
Elevation Gain: 3,028 feet
Rating: Moderate

Port Orford – April 22, 2021

The wind pushes against us as we pedal west. This was expected. The Cape Blanco headland, the westernmost point in Oregon, protrudes into the Pacific Ocean along a coastline known for its blustering year-round breezes. Why should we be spared?

A narrow road rises and falls as we pass cranberry bogs, a field with grazing sheep and gorse, an invasive shrub that glows with its clusters of bright yellow spring flowers. We proceed, lowering our heads against the gusts. Six miles in, the historic Hughes House appears on our right. Designated camping for touring hikers and bikers is to the left. Straight ahead, a towering white lighthouse glimmers in the noon sun.

After 47 miles of riding today, the Cape Blanco Lighthouse is our featured destination. But while the Wild Rivers Coast Scenic Bikeway takes us to the lighthouse and the ocean, I'm enamored with another segment, a squiggling, secluded, two-lane forest road that follows the Elk River inland to the Rogue River-Siskiyou National Forest.

Port Orford, an hour's drive north of the Oregon-California border, is part of a coastal region promoted as the Wild Rivers Coast to highlight the towns, local beaches, and rivers that flow to the sea on both sides of the state line. While the popular Rogue, Smith and Chetco rivers get most of the acclaim, the smaller Elk River captures us today.

We're here in late April when dry weather usually arrives first in Southern Oregon. We have a full cycling schedule ahead of us this year and Bob Cortright suggested we get started as early as possible. After more than four hours driving from the Willamette Valley and a night at the local Sea Crest Motel, we begin early from Port Orford's Battle Rock Wayside Park.

Waves crash on the park's wide beach only yards from Highway 101, a roadway that sweeps into town past local storefronts and leaves just as quickly as it arrives. The road is wide, very wide, despite allowing only one traffic lane in each direction. Near a bend sits The Crazy Norwegian's Fish & Chips, a small dinner shack where the food is fast and tasty. It's become a regular stop for us each time we come to town.

"The vibe is definitely irreverent if not crazy," owner Dianne Hosford says with a laugh. "I don't expect my employees to be super-serious about things. It's not supposed to be a serious dining establishment."

It's not. Wooden tables and chairs are positioned next to wood-paneled walls across two small rooms. Customers are likely wearing knit caps and jackets in winter and ball caps and shorts in summer. The Crazy Norwegian is predictable, Dianne emphasizes. "The formula works."

It's been working for nearly 30 years. The fare has been steady since Dianne became the fourth owner in 2014. The No. 1 seller on the menu is fish and chips. No. 2 is fish tacos. "It's old school coastal fish and chips here."

The restaurant fits well within the community. Port Orford remains a throwback of sorts on the Oregon coast. It's a small town by anyone's definition; the 2020 U.S. census counted 824 residents. Dianne calls it "the outpost."

"It's a little hub in the middle of nowhere," she says. "It's an agrarian economy with a fishing industry. And, it's old."

All is quiet on this weekday morning, but I imagine a steady stream of recreational vehicles must roll through here on summer weekends. The local economic base hasn't changed much over the decades.

"It's still fishing for the folks who live here full time," concurs Erin Kessler, the local bike shop owner. "And logging, ranching, cranberries, stuff like that."

Erin and her family relocated here from Alaska in 2008, seeking just what Port Orford has to offer. "We wanted a smaller town with a smaller population where everybody might have varying political opinions or social opinions, but everyone still talks to each other. We wanted our kiddo to be in a smaller school."

She opened Pineapple Express Adventures in 2017, a bike shop catering to mountain bike and beach-compatible fat tire bike rentals. It's also a popular repair and resource center for cyclists riding the scenic bikeway or following the 370-mile Oregon Coast Bike Route from Washington state to California, though she admits there's not much money generated from these passers-through. "I give a lot of free air and free advice, and I sell a couple tires here and there. I've got free maps for people who come in and I show them the best places to catch the [scenic bikeway] route if they don't want to do the whole thing."

Here's her free advice. Drive north to Elk River Road and skip 3-plus miles of uphill pedaling on Highway 101.

I get it. Some people rightfully are concerned about riding alongside the highway traffic, but we find the road shoulders sufficiently wide to provide a safe buffer. Patti Rogers, Bob, and I push away from Battle Rock at about 10 a.m., ready for a stern test. A stiff breeze blowing from the north adds a chilled, resistant headwind as we travel first along a quiet, residential street and then on the highway until we reach Erin's recommended starting point. With a right turn into the trees, we escape the wind.

This is Elk River Road, Coos County Road 208, and the Rogue River-Siskiyou National Forest. We will pedal 19 miles southeast along the river to our turnaround point at Butler Bar Campground. Drainage from the nearby Copper Salmon Wilderness area flows into the river's north and south forks and merge. Still, the river is neither wide nor rushing. With a few exceptions, this water lingers, flowing to the sea at a leisurely pace.

We pass a few homes as we begin on this secluded stretch of road, each house set back from the right-of-way. Traffic is minimal, only those who live here, are camping or fishing, or are on the job with the National Forest Service have a reason to be here. The road is in relatively good condition; several smooth patches cover potholes we encountered on the same ride four years ago. The repairs give us more time for river watching and less time worrying about tire damage.

When asked to name salmon habitats across the state, Oregonians likely would suggest the Rogue, the Umpqua, the Deschutes and even the Columbia River, but not the Elk River tucked away here on the South Coast. The river is not long; about 29 miles, national forest officials say. We efficiently click off the first seven miles and arrive at the Elk River Salmon Hatchery, an Oregon Fish and Wildlife operation along the river. An official state document states the hatchery is designed "to supplement natural production of fall Chinook in the Elk and Chetco Rivers and Winter Steelhead in the Chetco River, and to protect and restore wild populations of fall Chinook, Coho, and Winter Steelhead."

Ryan Gertken, a local hatchery technician, says it in simpler language. "We want people to catch the fish we raise."

The hatchery collects and incubates fish eggs to nurture and enhance populations. The fish are later released into rivers. There are two boat ramps at the hatchery for launching drift boats in the peak season, usually between November to April, Ryan says.

The hatchery, nearly eight miles from the highway, seems remote and perhaps a little distant for visitors but Ryan says that's far from the truth. Plenty of people stop by, some to fish and some to follow a self-guided hatchery tour. Others drive to the parking lot, unload bikes, and follow the same path we ride today into the national forest. "This is a very popular spot for the bikers," Ryan says. "They swing through here all the time. I see a lot of the same people, too. Some are seniors and some are families with little kids. They'll either park at the hatchery or start out by Highway 101."

Ryan lives and works at the hatchery, and regularly takes advantage of his location by heading out at 6 or 7 a.m. for a ride before his workday begins.

What's the appeal?

"The scenery. It's calm, it's quiet. There are plenty of pull-offs to hang out by the river. I usually have a snack at the bridge and watch the fish. That's kind of my thing."

I enjoy how the environment changes once we cross into the national forest. The road narrows and deep, lush green becomes a primary color. Trees, thick underbrush, ferns. We instinctively slow down as if we've passed through a gate and entered an enchanted wilderness. We move under the canopy and recalibrate to listen for the babbling river, chirping birds, and a much gentler wind wiggling leaves above us. We stop, as Ryan does, to watch water spill over rocks and flow down through an increasingly narrow gorge. Once calm in pools, the water turns emerald to the eye. We take pictures and marvel. There are many miles ahead of us, yet we're not in a hurry.

Eventually, we pass Butler Bar Campground and briefly stop at a small bridge spanning the narrow river, Ryan's snack spot. It's not unusual to see wildlife here both in the water and in the sky. Bald eagles glide above, the steelhead and salmon swim below. We listen and absorb, then return to the campground for our own food break before following the river back to the highway, the wind, and our ride to Cape Blanco.

Back at U.S. 101, we turn west toward Cape Blanco State Park and its 147-year-old lighthouse. It's not an easy ride. Shifting winds buffet us for five miles. There are rare escapes from the gusts as Cape Blanco Road passes through a stand of trees and over a hill before finally opening to the windy headlands, the lighthouse, and the ocean.

The lighthouse, constructed in 1870, remains the oldest existing beacon on the Oregon coast. The nearby Hughes House was built 28 years later for ranchers Patrick and Jane Hughes. Both the lighthouse and the Hughes home are normally open for tours, but these are not normal times. It's late April 2021 and public places remain closed to guard against COVID exposure. It wasn't always this way, of course. Bob, Eric Jacobson, Jennifer Donnelly, Elise Hendrickson, Robert Mansolillo, and I rode this bikeway in May 2017. We entered the lighthouse and shed our bike shoes with their metal pedal clips in order to safely climb a narrow, spiral steel staircase to the top of the 59-foot tower. Emerging into the glassed "lens room," we gazed across a 180-degree view of the Pacific Ocean, beaches, and coastline.

The focal point of the room is the lens itself, an assembly of thick glass surfaces 4 feet, 8 inches in diameter and 6 feet, 8 inches high. A 1,000-watt light bulb beams its signal to all the ships at sea every 18.2 seconds. That wasn't always the case. Lighthouse keepers James Langlois and James Hughes, the second son of Patrick and Jane Hughes, kept lamps fueled first by lard oil and then mineral oil burning inside the tower from sunset to sunrise for decades. Langlois, namesake of a small, unincorporated town 14 miles to the north, served as head lighthouse keeper for 42 years. Hughes, at first Langlois's assistant before succeeding his boss, worked there for 37 years. Oil burning ended in 1936 when the lighthouse was electrified.

Winds sweep the headland today. "Will you hold your jacket above your head while I take a picture," I ask Patti, hoping to capture the wind's intensity in a single image.

"How's this?" she yells so she can be heard over the rush of air. Her arm, at a 45-degree angle, isn't high enough.

"Straight up," I yell back.

She raises the jacket higher with her right arm and the current immediately pushes it horizontally pointing south. I hear the fabric snap as though it were a flag on a pole. A few seconds later, the wind eases and the jacket slumps then dangles limp. I got the picture.

The gusts make riding a bike on the steep, narrow path between the lighthouse and the road a challenge as it pushes to our right. We pass through a small gate and retrace our route back past the cranberry bogs and gorse, over hills and across small patches of gravel to Highway 101 and our return to Port Orford. The highway slopes downhill. After a three-mile, gravity- and wind-assisted descent, the directional scenic bikeway signs tell us to turn toward the ocean for a leisurely tour to Paradise Point State Recreation Site and then Port Orford Heads State Park. After one more ocean view, we return to Battle Rock and prepare for the four-hour drive home.

Jennifer couldn't make this trip to the South Coast. I thought it was unusual when she missed our planning meeting in January because she enjoys working through ideas with us. Then, in February, she sent unimaginable news.

"I have been delaying this email, but I wanted to let you all know what is going on with me, so when it comes to bike planning and trips you understand why I am a maybe or a no or not-sure participant," Jennifer wrote.

She explained that she had been diagnosed with ovarian cancer, and briefly outlined her chemotherapy schedule. "As you can imagine, this rocked my world to the core. I will try to join you to the best of my ability on shorter rides."

We're shocked and saddened yet buoyed by her optimism.

"Chemo is going better than I expected," she updated us in an April 5 email. "I am not halfway through the process. My energy level is pretty good, but my strength is not great. I ride at least 20 minutes every day—my health ride."

She remains upbeat and seems encouraged that she'll be back with us, we tell each other. We would expect nothing less from Jennifer, and we try to stay as positive as we wait to hear more about her recovery.

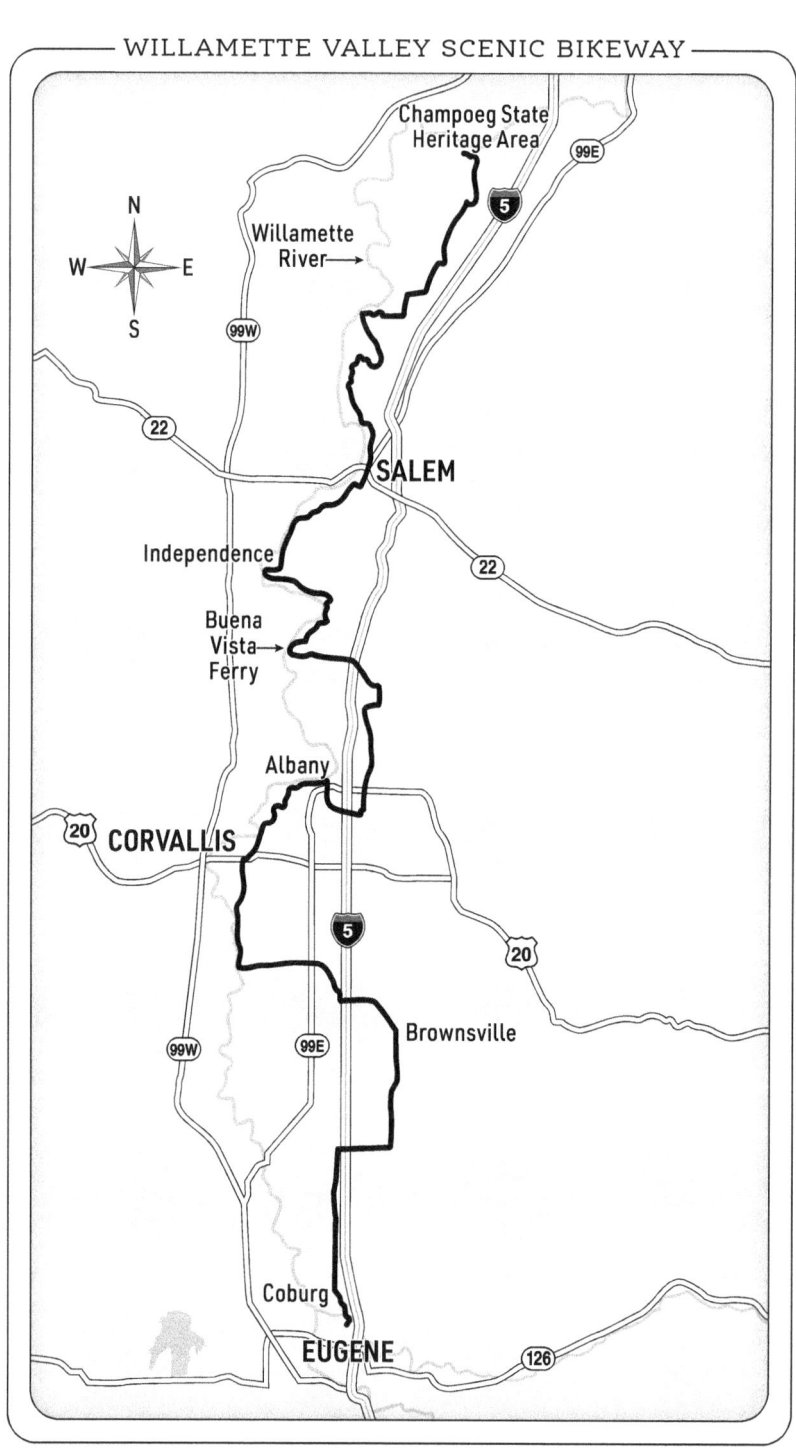

WILLAMETTE VALLEY SCENIC BIKEWAY

Champoeg State
Heritage Area

99E

5

N
W   E
S

Willamette
River→

99W

22

SALEM

Independence

22

Buena
Vista →
Ferry

Albany

20   CORVALLIS

5

Brownsville

99W   99E

20

Coburg

EUGENE   126

3

The First Bikeway
Willamette Valley Scenic Bikeway

• • •

Start and Finish: Champoeg State Heritage Area
or Coburg
Distance: 134 miles
Elevation Gain: 2,585 feet from Champoeg,
2,296 feet from Coburg
Rating: Moderate

Butteville – May 21, 2021

his is the indigenous land of the Kalapuya, native peoples
who hunted, fished, and gathered here for thousands
of years. Consider the Kalapuya a coalition of autonomous
tribes, some of whom with tribal names well known today for
the rivers and streams they once counted on as resources. The
Tualatin, Yamhill, Santiam, and Luckamiute were all considered Kalapuya people. So were the Tecopa, Chelamela, Ahan-
tchuyuk, Chenapinefu, Chemapho, Chafin, Peyu, Winefelly,
and Yoncalla.

They managed the land and gathered berries, nuts, and
roots. They roasted the bulbs of the camas lily that were dug
from the wet river floodplains. They also harvested wapato, a

marshland vegetable, and dried hazelnuts in the sun. This was their homeland, and estimates placed the population at about 15,000 people, according to the Oregon Historical Society.

That was until the white man arrived. Fur trappers appeared in the early 1800s and a trading post opened for business at Champoeg, now the northern terminus of the Willamette Valley Scenic Bikeway. A seminal moment in Oregon state history occurred at Champoeg on May 2, 1843, when valley settlers met to vote on creating a provisional government. "Wolf meetings" earlier in the year were arranged to discuss how settlers could manage predatory wolves, bears, and cougars that were attacking livestock. After creating a system to collect money and pay bounties for dead animals, it was decided a provisional government was needed. The vote was close, 52-50.

Champoeg bloomed into a small town of 200 until the Willamette River, the region's natural benefactor for centuries, reclaimed the land. Flood waters swept away the town in 1861.

The Champoeg State Heritage Area, a popular camping spot and day trip destination along the river north of Salem, commemorates this history. It's common to find people here enjoying a picnic, walking, biking, jogging, fishing, and even playing disc golf across its 678 acres. Oregon State Parks reports the park is used more than a half million times a year.

The scenic bikeway extends from here to Coburg, a small town north of Eugene. At 134 miles, this is one of the bike system's longest routes. Riders heading south pass through Salem, the state capital, as well as Keizer, Jefferson, Albany, Brownsville, and finally Coburg. They narrowly skip past Independence and Corvallis. It will take three days of riding to cover the distance.

The historic Butteville Store, billed as the oldest continuously operated retail business in Oregon, is now owned by the Oregon Parks and Recreation Department. Butteville, less than three miles east of Champoeg and accessible to us along a paved riverfront bike path, once was another docking point for traders in the early 1800s. The town grew with boat and stern-wheeler traffic over the decades as local crops, primarily hops and wheat, were shipped from this point. The advent of the railroad, however, led to a decline in river shipping and Butteville gradually evolved into a very small residential community.

Rose Owens joins us today as she tests her legs for three long Eastern Oregon bikeway rides later this summer. I surmise she may be testing me out as well. Rose and Patti are friends, but Rose and I meet today for the first time. I don't blame her for wanting to spend a day with us before agreeing to commit to a full week on the road.

We begin our day at the Butteville Store and ride the trail to Champoeg, crossing and eventually exiting the park. Road signs point toward 27 miles of open farmland before we reach the Keizer city limit, so I start taking note of the crops we pass. There's a field of grass waiting to be harvested for seed, and vegetables too small to identify by sight as we speed by. There are hazelnut orchards, and eventually the tall, long trellises of hops.

Our first stop calls for a snack and photos in front of the Saint Louis Catholic Church, a 141-year-old structure that served as sanctuary for a Jesuit enclave that began here in 1844 under the guidance of a missionary, the Reverend Aloysius Verecuysee. A log church was first built in 1845 and the parish formally organized in 1847, taking its name of Saint Louis from the era's king of France, Louis Philippe I.

The gleaming white structure on Manning Road today was built in 1880. It stands serene as we rest at the top of four concrete steps by the building's front door. Look north or south and the road's freshly painted double yellow lines are only interrupted by the shade of nearby trees blocking the late morning sun. No cars. No trucks. No farm machinery that typically passes this way. We sit a little longer if only to absorb the silence.

Manning Road turns to Keene Road which turns to River Road which turns to Matheny Road as we take 90-degree angles toward the Willamette River. Another turn, this time onto Wheatland Road, leads us away from the Wheatland Ferry, the first of two operating ferries near this bikeway. I pedal alongside Rose.

"Are your legs OK?"

"I'm feeling good. I think I'll make it," she says without emotion. I drop back, slide behind her back wheel, and glance into my mirror to check for vehicles that may be approaching. I look back up and realize Rose is feeling fine; in that brief moment she's accelerating and creating a gap between us. And, the gap is growing.

She wants to sprint away? I stand on my pedals and push hard to catch her. She relents and I once again roll beside her. Turning my head, I look into her sunglasses. She stares back as a sly smile emerges. We're no longer strangers.

The ride passes Willamette Mission State Park, the site of the original Willamette Mission established in 1834 as the first Methodist mission on the West Coast. Like Champoeg, this mission location fell victim to the river flooding in 1861. Our route eventually drops down and across the river floodplain's rich farmland before turning once more toward Keizer and Salem. We pass several nurseries along these tranquil, flat roads and watch columns of neatly aligned saplings visually click by like fence posts. Acres of flowers only inches above the ground create a palette of colors that gently dance in the north wind. There are more ubiquitous hazelnut trees.

The crops easiest to recognize from a distance are the hopfields with bines climbing like ivy up long strings to high trellises until harvested in late summer. I'm reminded of a 2016 trip to Italy during which my son Sam and I spent a day exploring Florence on foot. We stopped at a microbrewery called Mostodolce, a rarity in Italy then, for the novelty. A quick menu scan surprised us. One beer was described as brewed with "Willamette hops." The beer was excellent.

More than 170 crops are grown in the Willamette Valley, according to the Oregon Department of Agriculture. "I've heard numbers from 170 to 200 crops that are commercially grown in the valley," says Dr. Betsy Verhoeven, an instructor in Oregon State University's Crop and Soil Science Department.

Talking over coffee outside a downtown Corvallis coffee shop, Betsy explains what crops we might see while moving through the valley. She's well suited for the conversation. In addition to her scientific expertise, she grew up along the bikeway and has frequently pedaled here.

"The valley soils are largely from the Missoula Floods," she starts. "There's pretty fertile soil here, but it changes as you move south."

Imagine a series of tsunami-like events that sent torrents of ice, water, gravel, and most importantly, silt, into a lowland area. That's the Missoula Floods. Massive ice dams during the end of the last Ice Age—18,000 to 15,000 years ago—formed in what is now Montana, creating a 3,000-square-mile reservoir that geologists named Lake Missoula. These dams repeatedly broke and reformed, and each break sent hundreds of cubic miles of debris, ice, and water across the Idaho panhandle, down the Columbia River, and into lowland between the Coastal Range and Cascade mountains. This process repeated for nearly 3,000 years, creating an ancient body of water called Lake Allison. Those waters eventually drained north to the Columbia River and the Pacific Ocean, leaving behind the sands, clay, and silts that make the Willamette Valley so fertile today.

As a demonstration of the power of these floods, look to the Erratic Rock, a 90-ton boulder located near SW Oldsville Road south of McMinnville. It was deposited during one of the floods. The rock is composed of metamorphic rock argillite, according to the book *Oregon Geology* by Elizabeth L. and William N. Orr, and it does not match any other materials in this area. The scientific consensus is that this rock and others like it were encased in ice and erratically left along the floods' paths.

"There's also a lot of [deposited] alluvial soils from the Willamette River and tributaries. The river has snaked and changed a lot [since the Missoula Floods]," Betsy says. "Our biggest soil problem that limits what can be grown here is drainage. Wet, heavy, clay soils, acidic soils, and clay layers naturally occur that inhibit drainage. The biggest challenge growers try to manage is selecting crops that can thrive in those heavier and acidic soils, and the challenge seems to increase as you move south in the valley."

The northern third of this bikeway is an agricultural cornucopia.

The region is known for producing quality wine grapes at higher elevations, but Betsy focuses her work on what's grown on the valley floor. "I always think of the big three crops here being grass seed, hazelnuts, and other seeds," she says. "Grass seed and hazelnuts are definitely up there in terms of the acreage. Around 40 percent of the arable acres in the Willamette Valley, give or take, are in grass seed production. There are wine grapes, of course, and nursery production is huge, which I think is kind of under-seen by the public.

"But there's also quite a bit of specialty seed production, vegetables and flower seeds, sugar beet seeds. I've seen more and more garlic seed, too," Betsy explains. "There's a good climate for seed specialization here in the Willamette Valley with mild, moist winters and then we have dry summers, so things dry pretty naturally."

Some farmers post roadside signs telling passersby what crops are being grown, eliminating the guessing game. Other crops need no introduction. Blueberry bushes are easy to spot, strawberry fields emit an unmistakable scent after harvest, and there's that unique fragrance in the air when you ride downwind of a mint field on a warm day.

"The mint. Yeah, there used to be a lot more mint in the valley when I was growing up," Betsy says. "You'd smell mint everywhere, but there's less and less mint now because of diseases in the soil. Production has moved east to Idaho and then, even India."

We stop near Keizer to say goodbye to Rose who is detouring and heading home. We're enthusiastic about her joining us for a weeklong tour. In turning off the route, Rose skips the suburban ride through Keizer neighborhoods and bustling Salem traffic. The official route directions instruct riders to follow signs to the state Capitol building and south another mile through Bush's Pasture Park and eventually west to River Road South.

"As we worked through alternate route possibilities, taking folks through the Capitol grounds and Bush Park seemed like an attractive option," says Doug Parrow, a Salem cycling advocate and a member of the state scenic bikeways committee. "The consensus was to use the paths through Bush Park, which then prompted a search for traffic lights to cross Commercial and Liberty [streets] and to get back to River Road."

The circuitous route weaves through South Central neighborhoods and eventually makes its way to River Road. We prefer to go in a different direction, however, forgoing Bush Park in favor of a short downtown detour to Riverfront Park. The Peter Courtney Minto Island Bridge, a foot/bike bridge named after longtime state Sen. Peter Courtney that crosses a Willamette River slough, leads to Minto-Brown Island Park's 1,200 acres of grassy fields, woods, wetlands, and paved paths for bike riders, walkers, and joggers. Doug and the other bikeway planners didn't have this option when the bikeway route was finalized in 2009. The Courtney bridge opened in 2017.

We cross the bridge and slowly ride through Minto-Brown, carefully dodging families, small children, and dogs on long leashes. Detouring through the park eliminates more than four miles on busy streets. August excursions are slowed, however, by an invasive plant species that grows all over the valley. It's the Himalayan blackberry (also known as the Armenian blackberry), a plant believed to have been introduced here in the 1880s. While it's considered a noxious weed, it's a summer staple, thriving in these fertile soils. It's seemingly everywhere along roadsides, by farm fields, in parks, in the woods.

The park, a Willamette River floodplain each winter, is lush with blackberries. We closely watch the bushes throughout the summer, monitoring the berries' progress as they appear small and pink before maturing in the warm sun. Once the berries are full, dark, ripe, and easy to pick, we eat them. Lots of them, carefully slipping our hands between branches hoping to dodge sharp thorns until we pluck the plumpest and sweetest with a thumb and index finger. Empty water bottles are sometimes filled with berries and carried home.

Once we've had our fill of berries for the day, we push away and eventually emerge on the south edge of the park, reconnected with the bikeway. Back on River Road, we rise and fall with the undulating asphalt, pass under two train trestles and pedal into more prime farmland. The Independence Bridge is about a mile away.

Independence – May 22, 2021

We rode 45 miles yesterday and have another 43 ahead of us today, this time riding south from Independence through Albany and on to a stopping point on the east side of the river near Corvallis. Independence is not officially on the bikeway, but it should be. This agricultural community with its quaint downtown is less than a mile from the route and a perfect place for cyclists to start, stop, or simply take a midday break.

City officials know this and are taking advantage of the town's proximity to the bikeway as well as Polk County's rural roads, encouraging cyclists to visit, ride, dine, and stay the night here. They call it "Bike Indy Oregon."

Shawn Irvine, the local economic development director, says Bike Indy Oregon is the culmination of the city's efforts to create a community bike strategy during the past decade.

"The scenic bikeway bypassing Independence was disappointing in the sense that it felt like a missed opportunity, but it didn't trigger us to do more with bike tourism," Shawn says. Instead, it was the statewide tourism agency Travel Oregon that planted the seed. "We went to a few workshops and conferences, and they talked a lot about bike tourism as an area of opportunity. It made us look around at the assets we had to work with—flat, low-traffic roads, great scenery, even the bikeway since it was just across the bridge. It made sense to target bike tourism as a way to grow our local economy."

And they did, starting with the installation of a biker/boater campground near Riverview Park and the installation of bike repair and water bottle refill stations. Then they created brochures and online maps, and began promoting businesses as being friendly and welcoming to cycling customers. They also recruited organizations such as Cycle Oregon to stage bike events in town.

"Even though the bikeway bypassed Independence, it was a mark in favor of targeting bikes because someone clearly thought the Mid-Valley was a good place for bike tourism," Shawn says.

Independence became the cycling hub. A hotel, conveniently named The Independence, opened next to the city park in 2019 with rooms and facilities tailored for bike riders. Since then, Main Street has gradually transformed with new restaurants, breweries, sweet shops, and other storefronts appealing to visitors.

But it took a pandemic to create a name for it all.

The Bike Indy Oregon concept originated not as a tourism campaign but a way to motivate a community finally escaping COVID's lockdown. "Bike Indy was initially intended to be a locally focused activity to build a sense of community," Shawn says. "It was a way to get together with friends, meet new people, bond over bikes while getting exercise, that kind of thing."

The idea worked so well bike riders started arriving from out of town. Local businesses benefited. The community as a whole benefited. "We thought that was a great thing so we expanded our definition of community," he says. Bike Indy Oregon stages its own free events inviting cyclists on selected weekends. "And, it made sense to end the rides at a local establishment for drinks and good cheer."

Independence and nearby Monmouth, home to Western Oregon University, now host a variety of cycling events year after year. Eola Hills Wine Cellars, a few miles up the road in tiny, unincorporated Rickreall, has been showcasing Polk County cycling and wineries for more than 20 years with its Bike Oregon Wine Country events every Sunday in August. Some county roads lead past vineyards and wineries, some zip by hopfields, and some send us near the freshly cut mint.

Cycling is just as pleasant in Polk County as it is in Lane, Linn, and Marion counties. We head to the vineyards and Sarah Helmick State Park. We test ourselves on the "Stapleton bump," a short steep hill just south of Monmouth.

We often follow a Bike Indy route south to the hamlet of Buena Vista where the Buena Vista Ferry carries us east across the river. We walk our bikes on board, give the ferry pilot our $1 fares, and relax as the flat-top slowly crosses the water. Ospreys are nesting on the east bank. It's five minutes of peace; the loud, rumbling ferry engine becomes white noise. Once across, we walk our bikes up the ramp, pedal a quarter mile, and reconnect with the scenic bikeway.

No ferry ride today. Patti and I start from downtown Independence, cross the bridge, and pick up the official trail heading south on Riverside Drive. I know every rise and fall along this road, every bump, every crack in the asphalt. We emerge from a small stand of trees along the river into an open farm field passing row after row of blueberry bushes on our left. Hazelnut trees are on our right with strawberries growing between each row. We continue south under a train trestle and over a series of short hills, passing Ankeny Vineyard and skirting the edge of the Ankeny National Wildlife Refuge, a wintering habitat for geese and other migratory birds. It's typically quiet as we roll by; the Canada geese have flown on by the time we arrive each spring.

Past the refuge, signs for the ferry appear. We continue south, however, and head for the rural community of Jefferson, then on to Albany, the Linn County seat. We transition from rural roads and hay fields to residential streets and eventually downtown traffic. Storefronts line 1st Street as we approach the Albany Historic Carousel & Museum with its two-story, arched windows. Kids inside ride atop hand-carved horses, bears, rabbits, and fish as they rotate on the turntable.

Just as quickly as we arrive at the carousel, we're gone. Route signs lead us to Bryant Park and into the countryside once again for another 17 miles of quiet country beauty.

Coburg – May 23, 2021

We're reversing direction on Day 3, starting at the southern terminus for a ride back toward Corvallis. Out of the car at Armitage Park, 64 acres of Lane County land just south of Coburg, we begin the regular pre-ride routine. Lift bikes from the rack, check tire air pressure, nibble on energy bars, and place water bottles in their holders before finally securing and activating our bike computers.

Our task today is to ride the final 46 miles north. The weather forecast indicates a low chance of rain, but I question the weather calculations as we roll through Coburg, over Interstate 5 and head east. Dark clouds are forming directly ahead of us, pressing against foothills lining the valley's eastern edge. A tailwind propels us toward the threat.

The worst is straight ahead, but our road bends 90 degrees toward Brownsville in about two miles. I look to my left for my own real-time prediction. The sky over Brownsville is light gray, not dark. If we take advantage of this tailwind, we may be able to make the turn and avoid a soaking.

"I THINK WE'RE GOING TO BEAT THE RAIN," I shout to Patti as she rides about 50 yards ahead. She raises her hand. Did she understand me or did she think I was shouting "CAR BACK" as we always declare when a vehicle approaches from behind? It doesn't matter anymore because . . .

I feel raindrops.

We're now a half-mile from the sweeping turn and we've gone from sprinkles to drizzle. A little bit farther, just a little bit more, and we break away from the darkest clouds. And, as quickly as it started, the rain tapers back then finally stops. We enjoy a dry, downhill glide for three miles, turn left onto Main Street, cross the Calapooia River Bridge, and arrive in downtown Brownsville.

The streets are quiet this weekday afternoon. Randy's Main Street Coffee, our targeted stop, is housed in what appears to be a merger of two old buildings, one brick and the other wood frame. Larger-than-life-sized wood statues of Hugh and Clarissa Brown stand outside between the coffee shop and the Pioneer Picture Gallery, home to the community's pictorial history. The Browns, pioneer settlers and among the town founders, started the Brownsville Woolen Mills here with Thomas Kay and others in 1861. Historical note: Kay's three grandsons went on to create the famed Pendleton Woolen Mills in the early 1900s.

We're 24 miles into the day; time for coffee and calories, so we roll the bikes onto a gravel-and-asphalt patio area, find a table for two and relax. Two small Italian-style macchiato coffees and pastries are casually eaten under an emerging late-morning sun while a group of women, locals we assume, sit in the shade and converse over their drinks.

Proprietor Randy Ginn came to Brownsville in 1994 and opened his coffee shop two years later. "A friend offered me the use of a building and an old espresso machine and asked me 'Can you make something out of this?'" Randy recalls. "And I'm still in business in spite of myself."

I ask Randy about one of the town's claims to fame, the 1986 Rob Reiner film *Stand by Me*, a coming-of-age film that follows a group of boys in search of a dead body in the woods. Brownsville played the role of the fictional Castlerock, Oregon.

"You really need to talk with Linda McCormick."

Linda McCormick stands by Brownsville. If there's a volunteer cause in town, there's a good chance Linda is involved. "I just say 'yes' too many times," she admits. "My husband keeps saying 'can't you ever say no?'"

The McCormicks retired to Brownsville in 2005 from Southern California and she's loved it ever since. "I tell people I've never felt at home anywhere else," she says.

Linda is a member of the Linn County Pioneer Association. She's also an organizer for an annual Stand By Me Day staged here each July 23. When the date falls on a weekday, the celebration is subdued. When it takes place on a weekend, the film's devotees really show up. "We'll do a big thing because most of the people come from out of town and even from foreign countries," she says.

Celebrations typically attract 500 to 1,000 people. Nearly 4,000 people attended the 30th anniversary of the movie in 2016. Many of the day's activities take place in a park behind the museum. Antique cars from the era, the summer of 1959, may be parked downtown where many of the movie's scenes were filmed. And, of course, the movie is played on a giant, public screen.

"Everyone can pluck something out of the movie that they can relate to," Linda says. "It's a very realistic storyline, not necessarily a happy storyline because the kids are all going through some issues with homelife or whatever, but everybody seems to be able to find something that they relate to and it becomes a very personal kind of thing."

She recalls the time a fan visiting from Australia walked up to a post on the sidewalk, put his hand on it and declared, "I've waited a long time to touch this post."

"Someone once said that when you come here, it's like you're now part of that story. You're part of that movie. I can't explain it."

In one scene, the boys—played by actors Wil Wheaton, River Phoenix, Corey Feldman, and Jerry O'Connell—sprint across a trestle to outrun an oncoming train. There's no train dash on Stand By Me Day but there is a fun run. It's called the Ray Brower Memorial 5k Run and Walk. Why Ray Brower? Ray Brower was a character in the movie; Ray was the dead body.

With our coffee stop over and musical strains of Ben E. King's "Stand By Me" on my earworm loop, Patti and I pedal past the Hugh and Clarissa Brown statues and zigzag by the post office, the hardware store, and the Baptist church with its towering white steeple. We emerge into open farmland.

The route turns west toward the river then veers north, as we bounce across arduous chip seal pavement well suited for trucks and farm equipment but torturous for bikes. Chip seal is a technique in which road crews mix a layer of asphalt with one or more layers of aggregate rock. Larger rocks provide a more durable surface for heavy vehicles. Smaller rocks create a smoother ride. It's clear to us Linn County's road managers gave little concern to Peoria Road's scenic bikeway status. With arms weary and teeth rattled after six miles of rocky vibrations, we finally arrive at my car.

We received word this evening that Jennifer passed away yesterday. We await information.

I am without words.

4

'Wallets on Wheels'
Covered Bridges Scenic Bikeway

• • •

Start and Finish: Cottage Grove
Distance: 36 miles
Elevation Gain: 1,210 feet
Rating: Mild

Cottage Grove – June 5, 2021

Brownsville can lay claim to its connection with the movie *Stand By Me* but it's hard to top the movie credits compiled by the city of Cottage Grove. The city and its environs have played a role in several films including additional scenes of *Stand By Me, National Lampoon's Animal House, The General, Without Limits, Emperor of the North* and 14 other movies, television shows, or short films, according to the online entertainment database IMDb.

Animal House fans may recall the climactic "really futile and stupid gesture" when a college homecoming parade is sabotaged. Those scenes were filmed in downtown Cottage Grove. (The local chamber of commerce owns the movie's sinister-looking Deathmobile and uses it in parades.)

Silent picture buffs likely know about a famous scene in Buster Keaton's 1926 film, *The General*, when his production

43

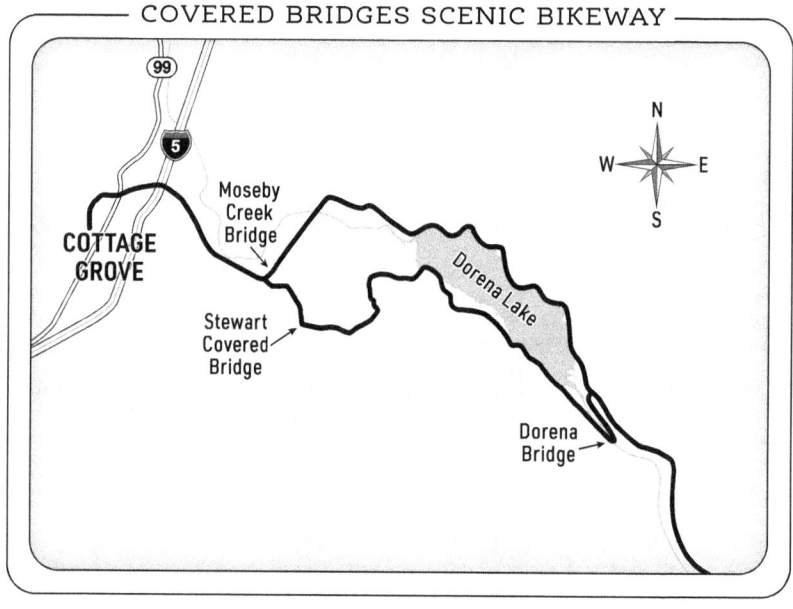

COVERED BRIDGES SCENIC BIKEWAY

COTTAGE GROVE

99

5

Moseby Creek Bridge

Stewart Covered Bridge

Dorena Lake

Dorena Bridge

N
W E
S

crew purposely set a bridge on fire and then sent a steam loco-motive across it. The engine, of course, crashed into the Row River below in keeping with the movie's plot.

And, the boys of *Stand By Me* hiked along the same railroad route 59 years later. Keaton's bridge was never rebuilt, but the red, steel *Stand By Me* bridge remains. Today that bridge supports bicyclists across Mosby Creek along the Covered Bridges Scenic Bikeway. While this span does not have a roof, it may be as famous as three covered bridges along the route.

This train path is now part of the Row River Trail, a 17-mile stretch of what once was the Oregon Pacific & Eastern Railroad line. The tracks were removed shortly after the *Stand By Me* scenes were shot here and the new trail eventually opened in 1998, running from the Mosby Creek trailhead east to unincorporated Culp Creek.

And, the Row River Trail is part of the Covered Bridges Scenic Bikeway.

Pronunciation Alert: The word "row" rhymes with cow. Legend has it two farmers engaged in a dispute over land, an argument, a row, according to Cottage Grove City Manager Richard Meyers. Blood may or may not have been shed. What we do know is the name stuck and now the Row River and Row River Trail are central to the city's cycle tourism industry.

Today's tour takes my wife Carla, my son Sam, and me from Trailhead Park east where we'll ride along the north shore of Dorena Lake and eventually to the Culp Creek Trailhead. This paved, multi-use path follows the abandoned railroad line next to the Row River and the reservoir. It's a pleasant, flat ride under the branches of tall firs and across open spaces. There are occasional rest stops with picnic tables and toilets. This may be the most family friendly stretch in the Oregon scenic bikeways system.

"The scenic bikeways are supposed to be the best of the best," says Richard, the local route proponent and a member of the state's scenic bikeways advisory committee, "and one of the things I was advocating for here was trying to get more family-friendly rides, the off-road trails where the recreational riders and the younger riders that aren't experienced can get out and have fun."

Richard sees the Covered Bridges bikeway as an introductory course for future cyclists and draws a local comparison to make his point. "The city runs the golf course here in town and one of the things we constantly look at is how can we get young people or people who haven't experienced this into golfing," he says. "Our current golfers are getting older and they're going to be leaving the market. We need to make sure we have others that are coming up behind them.

"I think cycling is the same way. How can we encourage people to learn and to gain the experience to the point where they can be riding the Blue Mountains [bikeway] or taking part in century rides and other things?" he asks. "It's so much fun getting out on our trail here and coming across a family having a great time with their kids on their little Sting-Ray bikes or BMX bikes. They may not make it all the way up to Culp Creek, but they may get to the lake. They may see a bald eagle."

We're enjoying ourselves, pedaling past Dorena Lake and on to Culp Creek, the end of the Row River portion of this route.

We take a break, munching on some food stored in back jersey pockets, before reversing directions and pedaling back four miles to face a choice. We can return on the same flat path or continue on the designated route to more difficult roads, hills, and covered bridges.

We go for the hills. Having unintentionally passed the Mosby bridge on our way out, we first come across the Dorena Covered Bridge at about 21 miles. This white, wooden structure, built in 1949, was erected as a way to cross the Row River after the creation of the nearby Dorena reservoir. The 105-foot-long bridge served its purpose until 1974 when a concrete span was constructed. The older structure was bypassed, and it now stands adjacent to the newer bridge as a monument.

The town of Dorena is underwater. The community that dated back to the 1850s and named for residents Dora Burnette and Rena Martin, was flooded by the reservoir. The town was relocated five miles east.

Our next landmark, the dilapidated Stewart Covered Bridge, appears eight miles later at Garoutte and Mosby Creek roads. It's worn out having been beaten by floodwaters, heavy snows, and age. Built in 1930, it closed in 1987. Both bridge approaches are gone.

We press on and return to Mosby Creek Covered Bridge barely a mile down the road. We missed this bridge earlier in the day when we followed the trail and crossed the steel *Stand By Me* bridge. We make the adjustment this time, riding about a quarter mile along Layng Road until the circa-1920 bridge appears ahead. Guardrails on both sides of this lightly traveled road funnel the approach to the one-lane span. The building's bright white wood contrasts against a green backdrop of firs and creekside underbrush. The open portal draws us inside.

We pause for pictures and then return to the Row River Trail for the final five-plus miles back and a quick loop downtown. There's one more span to cross, the Chambers Railroad Covered Bridge that local historians report is the only remaining fully covered railroad bridge in Oregon and quite possibly the only one west of the Mississippi River.

The Chambers bridge, built in 1925, no longer provides shelter for the trains. Instead, it's a point of community pride. The privately owned bridge across the narrow Coast Fork of the Willamette River fell into disrepair after it was retired from service in 1951. It was leaning toward collapse and only the strong, oversized timbers needed to support train engines kept it upright. The city acquired the bridge and adjacent land in 2006 and began a recovery project using grants, matching funds, and citizen donations. Restoration was completed in 2011.

Once across the Chambers bridge, the bike route turns north along side streets and passes over the river once more, this time across the J. Polk Currin Swinging Bridge, a wiggling, dancing suspension of wood deck and steel cables that force us to dismount and walk over the water.

Across the bridge and back on Main Street, we scan storefronts as we pass, looking for a dinner spot. The cozy Jack Sprats Restaurant is our selection, and it proves to be a great choice.

Richard Meyers calls cyclists like us "wallets on wheels." We represent how cycle tourism has become part of the city's economic development strategy, and on a larger scale how the scenic bikeways program is supposed to work.

"Yeah, we want those wallets on wheels to stop and experience what we have in our historic downtown," he says. "We have restaurants and brewpubs. When I came here 25 years ago, we were looking to paint bike lanes on Main Street but we had city councilors saying 'we don't want to paint bike lanes because it gets rid of parking spaces. They can just ride with the cars.'"

That's all changed.

"Once we got some of this work going and developed the trail and things like that, things completely changed on the council," he continues. "Now, the downtown people embrace it. We have the Oregon Gran Fondo [cycling event] every June. We've had criterium races. We have bike lockers downtown, and we look for ways to enhance it all and make it safer for cyclists. Councilors are eager to try to make sure that what we do on the roads accommodates bicyclists as well."

MADRAS MOUNTAIN VIEWS SCENIC BIKEWAY

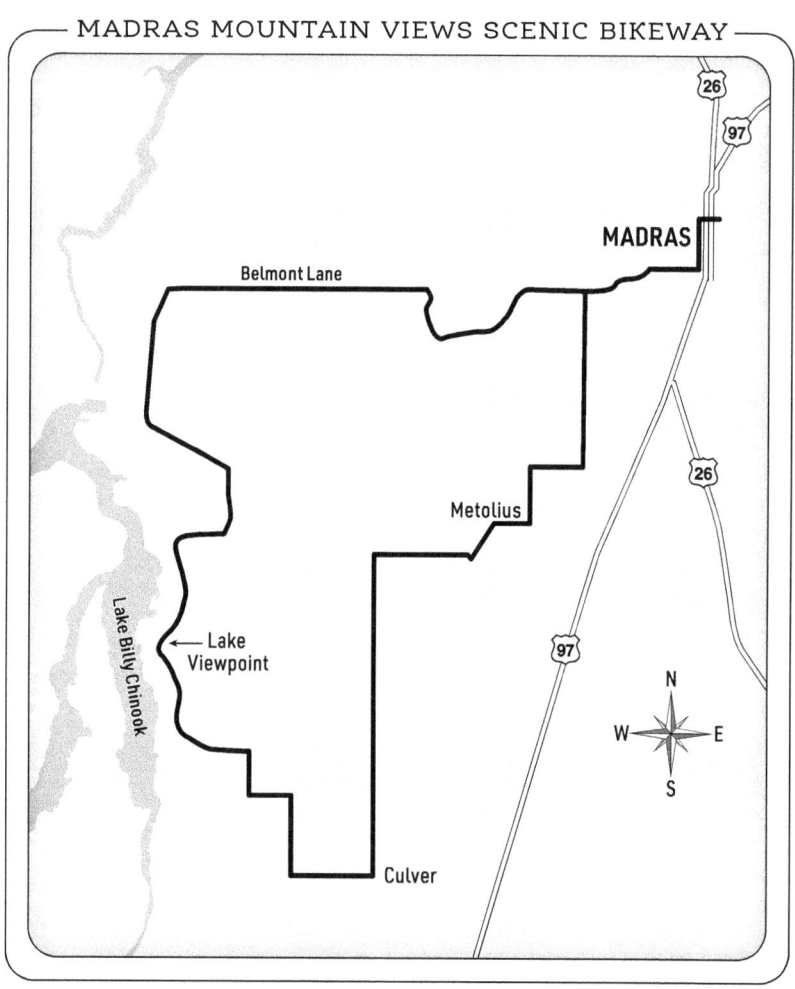

5

Staring Down on Billy Chinook
Madras Mountain Views Scenic Bikeway

• • •

Start and Finish: Madras
Distance: 29 miles
Elevation Gain: 1,175 feet
Rating: Moderate

Tumalo State Park – June 9, 2021

Central Oregon is sometimes considered Oregon's playground and it's clear the state's scenic bikeway planners wanted to take advantage of the high desert geography. Portions of six bikeways, some more difficult than others, fit within a 40-mile radius of Madras. We head over the Cascades today ready to test ourselves.

Eric Jacobson and Elise Hendrickson are driving from Portland while Patti Rogers is crossing the Santiam Pass from Salem. Carla and Sam are here, and Bob Cortright will arrive in two days. We're establishing a base camp at Tumalo State Park north of Bend where we've reserved three campsites for several days. We have plans.

We'll start in Madras, 42 miles north of the campground, for a pleasant, relatively easy ride on the Madras Mountain Views Scenic Bikeway. Day 2 sends us northeast 47 miles to Prineville and the Crooked River Canyon Scenic Bikeway. One of my favorite routes, the McKenzie Pass bikeway, is scheduled on Day 3. That starts in Sisters, only 16 miles from the state park.

While the other riders are sleeping in tents on the hard, cold ground, Carla, Sam, and I are camping family style in a yurt. Not all Oregon state parks have yurts; Tumalo has seven. We are fortunate to have secured an early reservation. This is a first for us, and we're living a few days of relative luxury. There's a futon double bed and a bunk bed in here. Mattresses are provided. We simply roll out the sleeping bags and our beds are made. Then there are basic comforts—electricity, lights, and heat. While heat is not needed in June, lights and power outlets to charge phones, bicycle GPS devices, and other accessories are never taken for granted.

The yurt itself is cylindrical with heavy canvas walls, a wood floor, domed roof, and plenty of vertical space to stand and move around. A one-step stoop outside the door provides a place for dusty shoes. This is more a canvas cabin than a tent. All cooking is done outside; it is still considered camping, after all. Bathrooms and hot showers open 24 hours a day are about 75 yards away. There is no Wi-Fi, not that we expected it. Wi-Fi is not provided in Oregon's state parks.

Once settled in, Sam and I take a walk under the park's canopy of Ponderosa pines. There are 54 tent sites here plus the yurts. A hiker/biker camp, a designated area for people without a motorized vehicle, is available. There's an $8 per-person, per-night fee for hikers and bikers, and spots are available on a first-come, first-served basis across a shared 30-by-50-foot space. A park ranger says the shared site can accommodate eight people from May through September and it rarely fills to capacity. Hot showers are available for these campers as well.

Our meal strategy is simple. We cook breakfasts, carry bike food (protein bars, a banana, trail mix or perhaps figs) for lunch, and dine out each evening. We're not far from Bend-area restaurants, and I'm not interested in campsite cooking after a long day on the bike. We drive into the nearby town of Tumalo the first evening where we find a collection of food trucks at The Bite on Cook Avenue. A local band covers country rock songs while we wait for our Thai dinners, then it's back to the campsite. We have an early wake-up call.

Madras – July 10, 2021

We rendezvous this morning at Sahalee Park in downtown Madras. With tires pumped, we start minutes before 10 a.m., heading south out of Madras and through the towns of Metolius and Culver. Metolius originally was a railroad town organized in 1911 by the Oregon Trunk Railroad. More than 1,700 people lived here at one time. The population is now barely more than 1,000, according to the 2020 U.S. Census.

Jefferson County, with Madras as its county seat, is a high plateau. It is open range. We pass mile after mile of wheat fields as we reach Culver and turn 90 degrees into a strong headwind that makes this flat road much more difficult as we continue, pushing west, then north, then west, then north making 90-degree turns until we reach a gravel path. A thick layer of small rocks forces us to dismount and walk our bikes perhaps 50 yards until we find a small lot rimmed by a thigh-high stone wall. Steep, scoured cliffs are visible across a wide canyon. Beyond them are snow-covered mountain peaks in the western distance.

After gently propping the bikes against the wall, we peer over a ledge to behold Lake Billy Chinook below us, its watercolors transitioning between green and blue. Were we to look up, we'd see Mount Jefferson dominating our line of sight. We would notice Mount Hood standing to the north. And, there's Mount Jefferson, Three-Fingered Jack, Mount Washington, the Three Sisters, Broken Top and Mount Bachelor. But we don't look up right away. We're mesmerized by our discovery in the canyon.

The views are captivating; no one is in a hurry to move on and this lookout quickly becomes our lunch stop. Everyone reaches into their back pockets for their foods of choice. I crave the banana I left in the car and settle for a peanut butter bar. The conversation eventually turns to the mountains, the remaining miles ahead, and this evening's dinner plans, but we keep coming back to the water. Small figures move across the surface extending thin, white wakes as they go. These are fishing boats, but from this vantage point they seem smaller than ants across a sidewalk.

There's no sense of urgency. This is the halfway point of our 30-mile ride, and we intend to enjoy it.

Lake Billy Chinook is a reservoir created in 1964 when the Round Butte Dam was constructed at the north end of three canyons. Waters from the Crooked, Deschutes, and Metolius rivers were blocked, flooding the canyons. Looking at a map, the lake takes on the look of a misshaped human body. The Deschutes and Crooked extensions look like legs stretching south to north while the Metolius points an arm far to the west.

Named for a member of the Wasco tribe who joined the John C. Fremont expedition in 1843, the reservoir covers 3,916 acres, according to the U.S. Forest Service. Splitting the Deschutes and Crooked rivers is Cove Palisades State Park. There's largemouth and smallmouth bass down there plus trout, kokanee salmon, and a few other species.

Once again underway, we head east on Belmont Lane. Eric rushes ahead to find an advantageous photo position as the rest of us climb a small hill. Eric possesses a photographer's eye and seeing an opportunity, he breaks away to find the best spot for a good image. Now, straddling his bike by the side of the road, he captures each of us as we crest the hill. I look over my shoulder, curious to see what he saw. There's Mount Jefferson dominating the frame behind us.

We make quick time from this point on. Like horses heading for the barn, we sense the end of the ride and quicken the pace. Five of these final seven miles are downhill, and we glide into Madras, zigzagging for a few blocks through town and back to Sahalee Park.

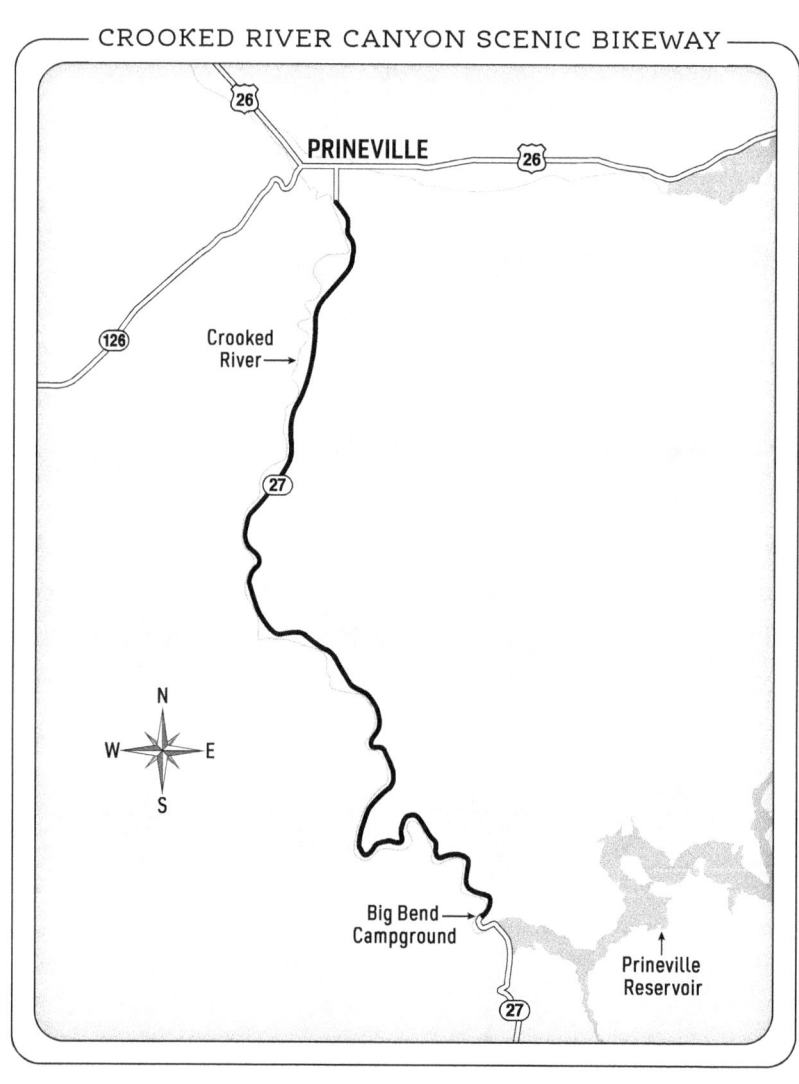

CROOKED RIVER CANYON SCENIC BIKEWAY

26

PRINEVILLE

26

126

Crooked
River →

27

N
W   E
S

Big Bend →
Campground

Prineville
Reservoir

27

6

'A Metaphor of Life'
Crooked River Canyon Scenic Bikeway

• • •

Start and Finish: Prineville
Distance: 18 miles one way
Elevation Gain: 728 feet
Rating: Moderate

Prineville – June 11, 2021

I wake up early, as is my habit, and start the day with a hot cup of coffee at the picnic table. Inhaling the aroma, I gently savor my first warm taste. As the minutes pass, I watch the state park slowly come to life. At first, the only movements are occasional campers walking toward the bathroom/shower building. A woman wearing a heavy sweatshirt, hood pulled over her head, walks with her dog a few minutes later. With time, this ad hoc community bustles with activity. Carla and Sam appear from the yurt and I begin preparing breakfast on the Coleman camp stove by 7 a.m.

Rumor has it Eric is cooking scrambled eggs with smoked salmon two campsites away, but the menu at Camp Yurt is pancakes, bacon, and fruit. We settle around the table, enjoying the hot food before it cools off. Carla and Sam then clean up while I prepare the bikes for Day 2: Prineville and a ride along the Crooked River.

Prineville is on the rise, thanks in part to Facebook establishing a massive data center there in 2010. Meta, the parent company of the social media giant, says it has invested more than $2 billion in the initial construction and subsequent expansions here. About 1,000 workers helped build the facility at peak construction periods and now about 350 people work there. Crook County is now the fastest-growing county in the state, due to the booming industry and relative affordability compared to its neighbors in the region.

We pull into Rimrock Park on Prineville's south side, ready ourselves and pedal south on Highway 27, the Crooked River Highway, crossing plateau pastures before dropping into the Crooked River Canyon. The river here is narrow and tame before it flows north to Lake Billy Chinook. We slowly split into two groups. Carla, Patti, and Elise ride ahead while Eric, Sam, and I bring up the rear. The sky is growing dark and soon we get our first raindrops. It's going to be one of those days.

For the record, the Crooked River Canyon Scenic Bikeway is listed at 18 miles, but that's only one way. Unless plans are made to have a vehicle waiting at Big Bend Campground near Bowman Dam and Prineville Reservoir, there's a mandatory ride back to town. That means total elevation gain is slightly more than 1,200 feet round trip, though still an easier day on the bike compared to other bikeways.

We make our way into the canyon. Basalt cliffs rise on both sides of the road as we follow the river that carved this path during the past 9 million years. Droplets hit my helmet and spot my glasses as the rainfall increases. I try to focus on our location instead of our condition, but it's time to get out of the rain. The problem is there's no obvious shelter out here. That is, until we look ahead and see the others huddled under the branches of a lone pine tree by the side of the road. This is not hard rain and it doesn't threaten our day. This break about 10 miles into our ride gives us a chance to eat, drink, and chat while we wait.

The Crooked River flows along the right side of the road as we head south. On a sunny day, we might see people walking along the riverbank intensely staring at their feet. They might bend down and use a small hand rake to comb through the rocks, turning stones over for inspection. We might see Jon Patrick, a 41-year-old commercial construction supervisor from Bethlehem, Pa., who spends vacation time walking along the banks of the river in search of agates, jaspers, obsidian, petrified wood, basalt, opal, and Oregon's prized find: thunder eggs.

Jon is a rockhound, a collector of stones. He hunts, collects, polishes, displays, and celebrates his finds. He's known to walk these riverbanks with friends from Prineville, collect his discoveries and stash them in a backpack. By day he'll explore rock exposed by road cuts and by night he'll camp by the river. This is what rockhounds do.

"We'll park along that road and pick through the gravel," Jon says.

Rockhounds do it in large numbers here in Crook County, the unofficial rock hunting capital of the world. "I've been there twice and I'm planning another trip in the spring," he says. "I've been up and down the West Coast and this is my No. 1 spot."

How did all these rocks get here? It's all about the local geology, experts say. Volcanism, active volcanoes, once dominated this land and the proof is evident on nearly every state scenic bikeway if you know what to look for along the way. The plateaus of Central Oregon? Basalt and ash. The jagged rocks atop the McKenzie Pass? More basalt. The rocks Jon Patrick travels across the country to collect are created by volcanoes and the gaseous liquids within.

Moving land masses and volcanoes are central to Oregon's geology, says Professor Sheila Alfsen at Portland State University. About 240 million years ago, one might say the Pacific Ocean beachfront was along what we now call Idaho. There was nothing here but water. Then things started to happen. A volcanic land mass that had formed in the ocean slowly moved east through the motion of plate tectonics until those rocks bumped into Idaho. Another mass, this time from Asia, did the same. Now together as one, this new terrane, accreted or attached to the Idaho coastline. Geologists call that the Blue Mountains. Next came the Klamath Mountains in much the same way, moving east until it also glued itself to the growing continental land mass.

That prompts a question: How could the Klamath Mountains be connected to Idaho and now be in southwestern Oregon? The short answer: Earth's crust stretched and pushed the mountains back to the west.

A more complex answer comes with the term *extension*, according to Elizabeth L. and William N. Orr's *Oregon Geology*. Heat from molten magma rose through the Earth's mantle, causing the crust to crack and break into rifts. The rifts allowed the crust to extend or stretch, pushing the Klamaths west.

While this extension was taking place, the stretched land separated into sections or blocks. Some blocks sank while others remained in place, forming what is now called the Basin and

Range region in south and southeastern Oregon. Look for evidence of this east of Lakeview. Shallow lakes remain where Ice Age glaciers once spread across the sunken zones. Lands that did not drop down now stand as mountain ranges. Hart Mountain in Southern Oregon, about 30 miles east of Lakeview and a visual landmark on the Oregon Outback Scenic Bikeway, is an example. The Steens Mountain farther east is another.

While what would eventually become Southern Oregon was extending, shifting, and sinking, volcanoes to the northeast began erupting. Lava flowed across much of what we now call eastern and north-central Oregon. More lava oozed from east to west through the Columbia Gorge across northern Oregon and southern Washington. This continued for millions of years. Eruptions, lava, ash, time. Repeat.

The Cascades volcanoes then erupted in two waves. Early activity appears today in the form of the lower foothills on the mountain range's western slope. A second series of eruptions created the larger Cascade mountain peaks we know today.

The thunder egg, a prized find in Crook County, is a collectable byproduct of this geology. It's a rough, bumpy geode rock with a gray or brown exterior that is scattered across this land. There's no way to know what's inside until you crack it open like an egg and discover a cavity filled with crystalized silica. Mineral impurities add unique colors and patterns, and the most attractive specimens can sell for hundreds of dollars. The thunder egg has been the official state rock since 1965.

And, the thunder egg, in a way, represents what Jon Patrick loves about rock hunting. "Once you start getting into this, you realize it's calming, it's soothing," he says. "It's kind of like a metaphor of life. From the outside, it looks rough. But you don't know what you will find until you see what's inside. That's what matters."

The rain stops and we're on our way. The river twists and turns and the roadway follows almost every bend for about seven miles from Castle Rock Campground to Big Bend. There are more stunning river views in Oregon, the Columbia Gorge ranking at the top of the list, but the Crooked River looks very good to me today as the sun breaks through the clouds and shimmers off the water. I stop, pull my phone from a jersey pocket and start taking pictures. Eric is doing the same thing about 100 yards ahead of me.

Yet another place to celebrate this land's natural beauty.

We expedite our return. Anxious to make fast time, we form a paceline. One person rides at a fast speed while others keep close behind in single file, each drafting on the person in front of them. The physics are simple: A single bicyclist faces wind resistance when riding alone. If a trailing rider can tuck behind the person in front, the passing wind is displaced by the leader and the follower takes advantage of the void. It's called riding in the slipstream.

A cyclist enjoying the slipstream advantage can move at the same speed as the leader while exerting about 70 percent effort. As the paceline moves ahead, each person takes a turn in front before gliding to the side and joining at the back of the line. The next person assumes the lead. Our process is repeated again and again as the final miles quickly pass.

The Top of the Cascades
McKenzie Pass Scenic Bikeway

• • •

Start and Finish: Sisters or Belknap Springs
Distance: 38 miles one way
Elevation Gain: 2,367 feet from Sisters,
3,876 feet from Belknap Springs
Rating: Extreme

Sisters – June 12, 2021

There are three primary ways to drive over the Cascades in Oregon. Highway 26 passes by Mount Hood and is the best option for those driving to and from metro Portland. Highway 58 extends east from Eugene and crosses the Willamette Pass. Santiam Pass is the route of choice for those traveling between the Mid-Willamette Valley and Bend.

The McKenzie Highway, on the other hand, is a two-lane road over the mountains that closes for months each winter once the snow falls hard and deep. That's our road today.

I'm excited every time I prepare to climb McKenzie Pass. I've pushed myself to the summit several times, each journey becoming a personal endurance challenge. No one is measuring my performance except myself. No one cares if I'm fast or slow.

Bob arrived at the state park last night and is ready to join

MCKENZIE PASS SCENIC BIKEWAY

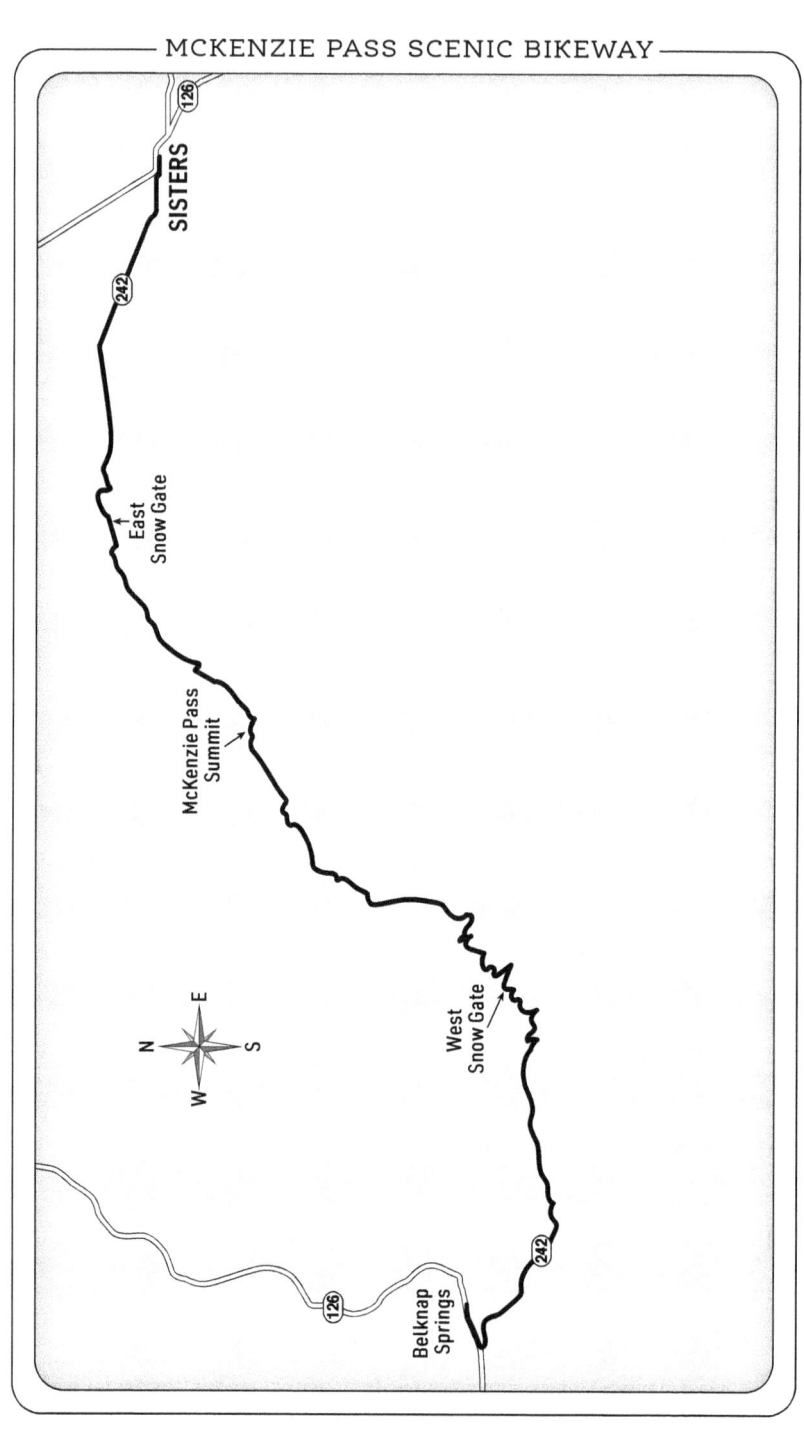

SISTERS

126

242

East
Snow Gate

McKenzie Pass
Summit

West
Snow Gate

N E
W S

242

126

Belknap
Springs

us for the McKenzie Pass Scenic Bikeway. We gather at Village Green Park in the center of Sisters, a popular town for day visitors just east of the Santiam Pass on Highway 20.

Village Green Park is unique in that two scenic bikeways start from here. We'll head west today and return another time to ride the Sisters to Smith Rock Scenic Bikeway.

Brad Boyd, owner of Eurosports bike and ski shop here, says some people refer to Sisters as "Mayberry in the Mountains" in deference to the 1960s TV sitcom *The Andy Griffith Show* and its fictional Mayberry, N.C. All was homespun, mid-20th century Americana in Mayberry. It was apple pie.

Sisters fashions itself as the quintessential western town from its downtown architecture to its annual Sisters Rodeo each June. Sisters High School uses "Outlaws" as its moniker. "This is a relatively small town," Brad says. "There were about 600 people here when we opened [the shop in 1989] and now, who knows, we have about 3,000. It's still a small town, still very neighborly."

This also is a tourist town, says the former mayor. Shops and restaurants invite visitors to stroll its main street, Cascade Avenue, most weekends. "But it's also a mountain town. We've got great access to the lakes. We have skiing in the winter, and we have great access for mountain biking and road biking."

Eurosport, located only a block from Village Green Park, is open for anyone needing bike equipment or repairs. To the side of the yellow, wood-framed building with its long front porch is a food truck pod and a beer garden, a gathering place after a ride up the mountain.

Business is good today. The McKenzie Highway, Highway 242, has been closed for several months and remains so until state road crews could clear snow and debris from the roadway.

And, while the highway is still closed to all vehicles including bicycles until the third Monday in June, cyclists like us descend on the city anyway. We all bypass the snow gates and ride before the highway is open.

The Oregon Department of Transportation (ODOT) recognizes that this happens every June and emphasizes that cyclists who ride before the road opens "do so at their own risk." But ODOT does nothing to stop the practice.

We monitor Brad's store website where he posts updates each spring on ODOT's progress clearing the snow. When he reports the roadway is clear, we ride. "There may be 200 to 500 people when we have good weather on a weekend day in late May or June," he says. "It's like there's a cycling event going on but, of course, it's free. And it's really cool."

The ride from the park is easy and casual as Bob, Eric, and I make our way out of town and onto the long, straight, two-lane highway. We're in no hurry; we've been up this road before and we know what to expect. Patti and Elise decide to drive to a picnic spot just below the East Snow Gate, trimming about eight miles off the ride.

Irrigated grazing fields transition to scrub, sagebrush, and Ponderosa pines and eventually basalt rock. People associate Oregon with rain but much of that precipitation stops on the mountains' western slope, leaving places like Sisters in what is called a rain shadow. There's snow here in winter but precious little rain the rest of the year. While it's dry and clear in Sisters on this June morning, we may see snow on the ground once we reach the summit.

Back together at the snow gate, we start the climb in earnest. Bob and Eric quickly pull away while Patti, Elise, and I ride at our individual paces staying in sight of each other until we reach the rugged basalt. The ride up this eastern slope is not dramatic, and my uphill speeds range from 5 to 8 mph depending on the steepness of the road grade. Both Patti and Elise are faster today, disappearing ahead of me behind mounds of dark gray and black rocks. I can't worry about them; I keep the pedals spinning and maintain my steady pace.

Entering a series of S-turns, I know from previous trips that the summit is near, a half mile to be exact. Snow piled on the side of the road is slowly melting; water drains from the base of each snowbank, flowing at a trickle across the pavement. Snow already has disappeared from some of the basalt, creating a mono-chromatic landscape of bright whites and shades of rocky gray.

There are three primary types of basalt lava flows: pillow, pahoehoe, and a'a. Pillow, the most common type, is rounded and looks much like, well, a pillow. It's seen throughout Hawaii. Pahoehoe basalt, prevalent in Eastern Oregon, is hot and runny during eruption and dries smooth. If it cools too fast, it can break apart into jagged, blocky a'a rocks with planar surfaces and distinct edges. A'a basalt seems to be everywhere up here. Rocky expanses extend in all directions. The road cuts through the lava flow instead of around it. It's desolate and rugged. This is permanent evidence of the Belknap Crater, the youngest volcano in the Cascades that erupted only 1,500 years ago.

I'm tired yet elated to reach the top once again. It's an odd juxtaposition. Snow is heaped by the side of the road yet the air temperature is in the low 50s. People are relaxing in short sleeves 5,325 feet above sea level. I find our group resting at the base of rock stairs leading up to the Dee Wright Observatory. They cheer my arrival as is the custom while I park the bike and grab a water bottle. I look south across the basalt landscape toward the Three Sisters mountain peaks. Their white caps point to the midday sun.

Built by the Civilian Conservation Corps in 1935, the Dee Wright Observatory is an open-air shelter and observation deck made entirely of basalt that provides a 360-degree view. I look across Mount Washington and Three Sisters wilderness areas. I can see the Belknap Crater and the cone-shaped Yapoah Crater that erupted nearly 1,500 years before Belknap. Interpretive panels explain regional geology as well as a few details about the travelers who first crossed the pass on foot, then by wagons, and eventually motorized vehicles. A sundial-like guide on the top deck serves as a compass pointing to each mountain peak. I wonder what early travelers would have thought of someone choosing to ride a self-propelled, two-wheeled device over the mountain for entertainment and exercise.

Rested and ready, we return to Sisters. The first nine miles downhill quickly click by, forcing weary legs to power through the final six before we see the park again. Even a flat road can seem difficult when you're tired.

Patti and I return days later to climb the west side. It's a weekday, and vehicles are still forbidden. We start from Belk-nap Hot Springs, a resort featuring two swimming pools fed by geothermal springs. This is the official western end of the McKenzie bikeway.

We head up Highway 242. The road is empty with the

exception of a stray camper van. A roadside readerboard signals the West Snow Gate: "Road Closed 11 Miles Ahead."

"We've only just begun," Patti sings, covering the first few notes of the Carpenters' 1970 song.

"Now I have a Karen Carpenter earworm," I complain minutes later.

"I can give you another song if you don't like that one," Patti offers.

I decline, countering as I often do with my bicycling earworm of choice. The Allman Brothers Band, with dueling guitar licks on "Whipping Post," rhythmically match my pedal strokes. I only need to slow the melody's tempo to my pace.

No matter the tune, I prefer McKenzie's western climb even though it's harder and longer. This is my HC, my *hors catégorie,* my big effort.

The term *hors catégorie* or "HC" is used in a grading system employed by the Union Cycliste Internationale (UCI), the international governing organization for professional cycling. The UCI rates mountain climbs based on a formula that scales degrees of difficulty. A Category 4 hill, for example, is the easiest. A "Cat" 3 climb is harder, a Cat 2 is harder still, and a Cat 1 is really tough. An "HC" mountain—*hors catégorie* in French means beyond categorization—is the most difficult, with measurements so extreme that they surpass the official scale.

We're not professionals, so we rely on the climb categorization established by Strava, a popular app among cyclists. While the UCI adds subjective factors into its scale, Strava's scores are purely based on numbers. Its algorithm calculates the road's average grade multiplied by its distance. The resulting number falls into a categorized bracket. There are minimum requirements, however. The average incline must be 3 percent or more and the ride from Sisters to the top of McKenzie Pass falls just short at 2.5 percent. The numbers for today's climb? 23 miles at 3.5 percent. It qualifies as an HC.

Other cyclists on the road today decided to skip the first 10 miles and begin at the Proxy Falls Trailhead turnout. Alder Springs Campground and the West Snow Gate appear two miles later. The road belongs to bikes alone the final 12 miles up to the summit. Around the gate and on our way again, serenity quickly flows over me. The forest is still except for the occasional chirping bird puncturing the relative silence. I hear my bike. I hear steady, constant breathing as my lungs seek more oxygen with each 1,000 feet of elevation gain. Patti quietly pedals behind me, then ahead of me, then behind me as we each progress within our own worlds, alternating positions up the mountain. We gain on and eventually catch a young bikepacker, his bike frame laden with bags. We offer encouragement; a few more miles and then the road begins to level off, we tell him. He grins at the prospect.

We pull to the side of the road for a drink of water and a view. Straddling our bike frames, we stand at more than 4,300 feet above sea level looking south over the forest. As we stand mesmerized, I recall something Brad Boyd told me: "The west side is just stunning. I never have a problem taking a break coming up the west side because you can stop and appreciate where you are and just listen to the wind and the birds in the trees. There's always another corner and another view."

He's right. Thin clouds appear like lace spread across a steel blue sky, towering Douglas firs stand as sentinels as the road switches back and forth below us. We see two bicycle riders making their way up. One level below us is the bikepacker, methodically pacing himself. Another level down is someone on a lighter, faster road bike pushing a quicker tempo.

The bikepacker emerges from around a curve about two minutes later. We invite him to rest with us and enjoy the view. He's heading east intent on reaching Iowa for the eight-day RAGBRAI, the Des Moines "Register's Annual Great Bicycle Ride Across Iowa," but first he must ride for more than a month to simply get there. We share more encouragement; he still has about 1,000 feet to climb over the next nine miles, but the first mile will be the toughest.

He's encouraged yet clearly tired. The summit can't arrive soon enough. Once there, we tell him, it's downhill to Sisters, the food carts, and a cold beer. He smiles.

The road continues to wind up and through this forest of firs and red cedars. We've covered this route in the past with and without traffic, but cars and trucks are not a concern on the west side of the mountain. Engines can be heard for miles as vehicles slowly accelerate, the sound rumbling up the hillside. And, with so many twists and switchbacks, drivers can't gain much speed.

The roadway starts to straighten, the gradient eases, and the basalt appears. We eventually pass a point where the Pacific Crest Trail crosses our path, and I think about the committed hikers who walk from Southern California to the Canadian border. I'm in awe. Finally, happily, we arrive once more at the summit. 5,325 feet above sea level, the sign says. Rest, food, and water are in order before we speed back down.

This is my favorite descent in Oregon. Those tight switchbacks that led us up now become our paved carpet ride down.

Patti speeds ahead through each curve with apparent abandon. She's a fantastic descender. While I'm cautious, in fact somewhat leery of speed, Patti flashes past deftly guiding her bike through the apex of each turn.

The adrenaline courses through me and the wind rushes across my cheeks as the miles pass by. The points of reference reappear and vanish in moments: our impromptu hilltop vista, the snow gate, Alder Springs, Proxy Falls. Miles of roadway quickly dissolve at 20-plus mph.

(8)

The Consummate Cyclist

Hood River – June 13, 2021

Our Central Oregon tour stops a day early. Jennifer Donnelly's memorial service takes place today.

Jennifer was our group's calm, steady voice of reason and a vital member of our riding group for several years. She was a friend, a bike route planner, a consistently strong cyclist, conversationalist, and subtle prankster. We rode many miles together.

We wanted to believe Jennifer would be back with us again soon and were encouraged by email like this: "Thanks for keeping me in the loop on the rides. I still hope to make it to some of them for shorter distances. I have had both my COVID vaccines so I may be a good candidate as a driver. Hope you all are enjoying the early spring riding. I will be outside riding my 10-mile loop soon. Cheers!"

She's getting well, we thought. That's why the news in late May was a shock. Jennifer would have loved to join us this summer. Her sense of adventure and camaraderie would have enhanced everyone's experience.

My relationship with Jennifer centered on cycling during the past five years. I learned over many miles about her career as a regional representative for the Oregon Department of Land Conservation and Development as she and Bob, a retiree from the same department, often talked about their work and what Oregon's statewide land use requirements had accomplished over the years. I knew she enjoyed international travel and that she volunteered for Crag Rats, a mountain rescue group helping those in trouble on Mount Hood.

As Bob, Eric, and I join Jennifer's family and friends to reminisce today at Crag Rats Hut near Hood River, her story comes into sharper focus. We were but a small part of her larger-than-life existence. She was a big part of ours.

Bob later recalls his first ride with Jennifer, one that started with an office conversation about their shared interest in cycling. Jennifer, he says, mentioned she rode "a fair share" and said, "you know, we should get together and ride."

"Then I was driving up to Hood River one day and I remembered Jennifer saying, 'if you're ever coming up, give me a call.' So, I thought, what the hell? I called her and I said, 'Hey Jennifer, we're going to be there in an hour and a half. Are you available? Do you want to go for a ride?'

"She said 'sure' and that was the start. She was an uber cyclist but that response to my call said more about her personality," Bob recalls. "We now know her offers were always very sincere. It was true to her sense of adventure. 'Let's go do it. Let's just go. I've never ridden with you before, but that doesn't matter. Let's go.'"

Friends at Jennifer's memorial service speak about her love for discovery, exploring destinations such as Morocco and Iran. Be it on a bike in Oregon or in an open-air market in another land, Jennifer relished each moment.

As friends share recollections, my mind drifts to my lasting memory two years earlier, the final ride during a three-day tour of Southern Oregon. Jennifer, Eric, Bob, and I had spent a long weekend riding around Crater Lake and along the region's backroads. We turned onto Butte Falls/Fish Lake Highway in rural Jackson County destined for a rest stop at Willow Lake County Park.

We had known this would be downhill, but we hadn't calculated the distance nor given much thought to what was about to unfold. Off we went picking up speed so quickly we didn't need to pedal. One mile. Two miles, still going. Another mile then another mile. Jennifer passed me and a moment later I overtook her before we eventually were gliding side by side. There was no traffic in either direction; the road was ours. I looked down at my speedometer and discovered we were rolling faster than 35 mph and gaining speed. Nervous, I reached to tap the brake levers. Before I squeezed, I looked to my right. Jennifer was staring to her left directly at me. She showed no fear, only a broad smile.

"This is fantastic," she simply shouted over the wind rushing by.

It wasn't what she said that struck me then and stays with me years later. It was her joy. She was in the moment, relishing the thrill every foot of the way.

That thrill went on for 10 miles. When it ended, we simply looked at each other and started laughing over a rare opportunity we shared. We were in that moment together.

Bob calls Jennifer the elastic that held our group together.

She would stretch ahead one day with faster riders and then choose to drop back and keep company with slower people the next. Off the bike, she was the rational decision-maker when indecision overwhelmed the rest of us. She was compassionate, never judgmental. She could gently poke fun to keep everyone at ease yet never jab at anyone's expense. She was the perfect travel companion, the consummate cyclist.

Eric Peterson, Jennifer's husband, tells us she always looked forward to our road trips, that each tour was important to her. "That's gratifying to hear," Bob says, "because we certainly got a lot from her."

That's how I remember Jennifer. The thrills. The compassion. The laughter. The moments.

The service ends. We extend our condolences to Eric Peterson and prepare to ride. No scenic bikeway today; we're riding east from Hood River to Rowena Crest, a vista along old Highway 30 with panoramic views of the Columbia Gorge. It was one of Jennifer's favorite spots. Once there, Eric Jacobson, Bob, and I hoist water bottles to toast the memory and spirit of our dear friend.

9

'A Professional Idiot on a Bike'
Painted Hills Scenic Bikeway

• • •

Start and Finish: Multiple locations
Distance: 161 miles
Elevation Gain: 12,864 feet
Rating: Extreme

Mitchell – July 6, 2021

We follow U.S. Highway 26 into Mitchell and steer the car onto a gravel parking lot along the south side of the road. Parking next to a small church, white with a burnt orange facade and a welcoming front door portico, we see a sandwich board sign that confirms our destination: Hostel Lodging.

The Spoke'n Hostel is a bicyclist's refuge along the Trans-America Trail, a 4,215-mile cross-country cycling route from Yorktown, Va., to Astoria, Ore. It passes right by the hostel's front door. People brave enough to ride across the country know the city of John Day is 69 miles behind them and Prineville is another 47 miles ahead. Mitchell, population 137, is circled on their map.

Bracing for hot weather, we come here to experience the Painted Hills Scenic Bikeway. This may not be the best time of year to ride in Eastern Oregon, but we've driven 200 miles to do this. There's no turning back.

PAINTED HILLS SCENIC BIKEWAY

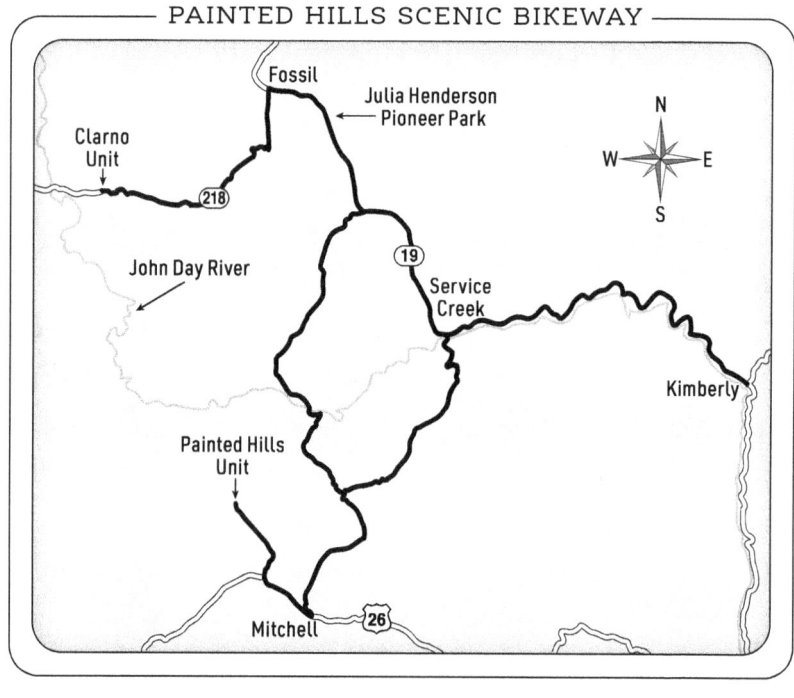

Jalet Farrell is at the door when we arrive, ready to greet Patti, Bob, and me with glasses of ice water on this hot afternoon. Everyone gets a cold glass and a tour, she says, starting with dormitory-style sleeping quarters in what once was a church sanctuary. Twelve beds, constructed from blue pine, stretch along both sides of the room in bunk bed formation, each with clean sheets, a blanket, and a handmade quilt. Every bed has a charging station for electronic devices. Cyclists typically park their bikes at the foot of their beds but only one, a 1980s-era Trek 870 mountain bike, is in the room today. Downstairs are two private rooms.

A table with bench seats covered by gold upholstery, perhaps reminding us of the nearby Painted Hills, is positioned in the center of the room. An upright piano with a wooden bench is to one side, waiting for a song.

There are showers with towels, soap, shampoo, and conditioner. Guests can soak tired feet in warm water and Epsom salt. There's a common room with a small library and comfortable couches; an oval wood table in the adjacent kitchen area seats eight. A coffee pot, teapot, and microwave are available and white ceramic coffee cups are set on a tray next to coffee-filled airpots. A refrigerator is at hand should we buy something at the nearby general store. In fact, this kitchen has everything a traveling bike rider could want or need. Jalet has anticipated it all.

Wi-Fi? It's here, Jalet says.

We arrive with reservations but most others, especially those riding the TransAmerica Trail, show up unannounced. All are welcome so long as beds are available.

Jalet and husband Patrick, both Assembly of God lay ministers, created the hostel in 2016 to provide affordable lodging and help support the local economy. Jalet organized a building remodel, moving the sanctuary to the common area for very small Sunday services. Jalet and Patrick say little about this being a house of worship. To them, this is a hostel first and foremost, a refuge where weary travelers can rest and rejuvenate.

We sit with water in hand, and I ask, "Why did you choose to cater to cyclists?"

"We didn't choose. It chose us," Jalet says, explaining how she had no inkling at first that so many bicyclists pass these doors. "I was fully entrenched in remodeling the building as a hostel. Then we found out we were 50 feet off the TransAmerica, so we focused on cyclists."

She shows us a photo of the bunk room during another group's stay. At least 10 bikes are propped upside down so riders can perform maintenance. "We're specifically set up for this. We're not worried about a greasy chain. We've got bicycle repair kits, pumps, and bike stands."

Economic research in 2013 commissioned by Travel Oregon, the state's tourism marketing agency, indicated people engaged in cycling-related activities were bringing more than $400 million to the state's economy at the time. That number is now approaching $1.3 billion by unofficial reports. "I thought if we had half a percent of that we would be OK," Jalet says. "I knew there was a potential for people to stay out here and, over time, those guests taught us what they needed."

She was right. About 350 people spent at least one night the first year and the numbers more than doubled every year since, excepting COVID-related declines in 2020 and 2021. And here's the surprise: The Farrells don't charge anyone. It's free. They accept donations and of the 3,000-plus guests so far, how many people have failed to leave a donation?

"There are so few I can count them," Patrick says.

Following Jalet's instructions, we roll the bikes to our private rooms and see she already has posted name tags on each door stating the rooms are "Spoke'n 4." We'll remove the tags when we leave and add them to a growing collection. That's Jalet's way of counting how many beds she provides over the course of a year.

Jalet modestly describes her efforts, making it apparent she's not interested in recognition. Patrick provides insight once she steps away.

"This [hostel] is what she does all the time, but Jalet doesn't see what she does as work. Hospitality just comes naturally to her," he says. "She just sort of exudes that."

I ask how the hostel fulfills their church ministry. "We believe that if you look at the teachings of Christ," Patrick says, "hospitality seems like the quickest way to get to the point that he was trying to make, which is love one another, right? And if you view it from that perspective of what does it mean to love someone that you've never met, well, then you start to look at what needs should be taken care of. Jalet asks herself 'what is it that these travelers are going to need.' You start thinking about that and pretty soon it just becomes really obvious."

"She's a good listener," Patrick says before correcting himself. "No, she's a great listener."

He recounts a day when a cyclist explained he was trying to recover after suffering a muscle cramp in his leg. "Do you have a rolling pin?" the guest asked, looking for a way to apply even pressure on the muscle. After retrieving the pin and seeing its use, Jalet recognized the need and quickly placed an online order.

"Just like that, we had muscle rollers," Patrick says, "and that's why I think she would downplay her role in this. She's thinking 'I'm just listening to what people want. That's all I'm doing.'"

So, is this her passion?

"Absolutely," he says. "Is it work? Oh, yeah. But you're right, it's her passion. We look through our guest book and read the comments. People say that everything they could think of from shower flip-flops to reading glasses has been provided. And it's funny because she says if you have everything you need to take care of bicycle travelers, you have everything you need to take care of any traveler. When you're traveling a long distance on a bicycle, you can't carry much."

Mitchell – July 7, 2021

We intended to get an early start ahead of the heat this morning but fresh coffee and the comforts of the Spoke'n Hostel have dulled our sense of urgency. We make scrambled eggs and fruit with ingredients purchased on the way to town and enjoy an extra cup of coffee while talking with other cycling travelers. We finally get started 45 minutes behind schedule. Weather forecasters said it would only reach 90 degrees today, a manageable temperature if we finish early in the afternoon. Fortunately, we have an air-conditioned shuttle strategy. As a safety rule, we keep our support vehicle with us in remote locations. To accomplish this, each of us takes a 15-mile turn driving the SUV, stopping every five miles or so to wait on riders and lend roadside aid, if needed. Today, we'll always have air conditioning only five miles up the road.

The Painted Hills Scenic Bikeway is a twisting design that has been described as a wheel hub with three spokes. I liken it to an octopus. A central loop forms the body and three roads create outstretched tentacles in different directions. One follows north to the Clarno Unit of the John Day Fossil Beds National Monument, another south to the Painted Hills Unit, and a third east between the communities of Service Creek and Kimberly.

The John Day Fossil Beds National Monument is made up of three separate locations or units spread across parts of three Oregon counties. The Clarno Unit is in Wasco County while the Painted Hills Unit is in Wheeler County and the Sheep Rock Unit is in Grant County. Combined, they make up one of the richest regions in the United States for geologic and paleontological research.

We drive nearly 60 miles north to Clarno, lather on sunscreen and start riding uphill. Minutes into the climb I sense the heat radiating from the road. It's only mid-morning. Why did we start so late? Why are we doing this in mid-July? Someone is going to suffer heat stroke. Where's the morning breeze weather forecasters promised?

I reach the summit after 87 minutes. (My Strava app later reports this ascent totals 10.7 miles with 2,119 feet in elevation gain, a Cat 1 climb. Slow and steady reaches the top.) Cresting the hill, we relish the cooling wind resistance as our bikes speed downhill toward Fossil.

Following a quick lunch at The Royal Stag, a restaurant on Fossil's First Street, we begin our next big climb of the day, a 10-mile, 1,100-foot grind up and over Butte Creek Summit on State Highway 19, the John Day Highway. We make our way up despite the heat with the misplaced belief we'll crest the climb, complete one more short bump and then enjoy another cooling downhill run.

Today's also the day we're reminded to never underestimate elevation profiles. It's an exhausting lesson. Elevation profiles are charts that commonly accompany cycling maps to show how much a road goes up and down. These horizontal graphics are quick visual guides. Perception is altered, however, when many miles are compressed into a small image. Detail is lost. What looks to be a short, small bump is, in this case, 307 additional feet of uphill work over a single mile with grades reaching as much as 8 and 9 percent.

We turn west on Rowe Creek Road and my spirits sag when I see the road begin to ramp up. I hear a pop-pop-pop sound as my tires roll across the narrow road's chip seal surface. It sounds as if I'm riding over small sheets of air-bubble packing wrap. Pop. Pop. Pop. I don't know the source; I've never heard this before. This can't be good, I worry, and I ask Patti as she rides beside me.

It's the asphalt, she says.

The asphalt?

Air and water vapors are trapped beneath fine aggregate rock during road resurfacing and they bubble up through the chip seal asphalt on hot days, Patti says and an ODOT source later confirms. Those bubbles then pop when bike tires roll over them.

"My husband is an avid road cyclist and he reports experiencing the same thing on hot days," the source says. "He claims that if you look close enough you can even see the small bubbles."

The thought of riding over boiling asphalt fogs my mind. I'm hot, very hot, and disheartened. And, now we have boiling asphalt. I enter a hairpin turn at a very slow spin rate and see Bob waiting with the car.

"Do you want to stop?" he asks in a supportive yet concerned tone. "Or, do you want to keep going? The top is around the bend."

That's what I need, some positive expectation that this anguish is about to end. My legs feel rejuvenated if only for a moment.

Bob is right. The road tops out about a quarter mile later and I'm now pain-free, gliding, picking up speed as the air once again rushes by me, cooling my body and whisking beads of sweat from my temples. I unzip much of my cycling jersey, hoping the incoming wind will help dry it out. Patti and I follow Rowe Creek Road downhill for a relaxing 12 miles until thick stands of juniper trees disappear. Grazing land and hay fields become the new landscape. Stratified hills and plateaus are visible in the distance. Bob drives past, moving ahead to the next meeting point.

Patti and I roll across the John Day River at unincorporated Twickenham after a few more miles. Bob is waiting there, parked under a lone tree for its shade. Thankfully, it's now my turn to drive. Patti and Bob ride away while I take time to rack my bike, change into a dry shirt, and eat a recovery banana. My work is finished for the day. I sit in the driver's seat and look at the car dashboard for the air temperature.

99 degrees

I roll up alongside Patti a few miles later to check on her welfare. We have two gallon-size jugs of water in the car, but her water bottles pinned in their bike frame cages appear sufficiently filled. She looks tired, but she pushes on.

"This is too hot," I say. "You should pull the plug and call it a day."

"I'm OK. I don't have much farther to go," she says, not looking up but instead staring down on the dreaded asphalt just beyond her handlebar. I reluctantly drive away. Two miles later the dashboard updates the temperature: 100. That's enough. We don't want anyone succumbing on the side of the road. I find shade, park the car, get out and look back in Patti's direction. She should be here any minute, I calculate.

Three minutes pass. No sign of Patti. Five minutes. Eight.

My mind wanders. Did she collapse under the heat? Did she crash her bike? I turn the car around and head toward her. Around a bend and only 300 yards away, Patti sits comfortably in the shade of a juniper tree. She's drinking water. She's fine. Still, I implore her to stop for the day. She's already made her decision. Enough is enough.

With another bike racked, we drive toward Mitchell and arrive at the hostel as Bob finishes his final 17 miles. We learned a hard lesson today: Get started earlier or don't go at all.

I'm reminded of something our hostel host Patrick said: "All you have to do here is roll your bicycle in, take a shower, check your email, go get a beer at Tiger Town, and then come back and sleep."

Good advice. Showered, dressed, and hungry, we stretch our legs with a quarter-mile walk down the street to Tiger Town Brewing Co., the name evoking Mitchell's rough-and-tumble history of gold miners, saloons, and gunslingers. The last gunfight here took place in the early 1900s, locals say. If you wanted a shot of whiskey, a poker game, or companionship back then, you visited the Tiger Town district. The town's upstanding, law-abiding citizens kept their distance, living up on nearby Piety Hill.

Tiger Town in the 21st century is tame. Brewmaster Shawn

Hawkins stands by the large bar inside the brewery/restaurant's dining room that was handcrafted by co-owner Robert Cannon. The building was once a tire store operated by Robert's grandfather. A red food truck positioned outside is the brewpub's kitchen because, after all, tire stores were not designed with kitchens.

For us, Mitchell is our oasis and Tiger Town is the watering hole.

Stand along Main Street outside the brewery and look to your left. Now look to your right. That's your tour of the local business district. Most of the buildings on Main Street are wood-frame structures and there's an Old West architectural vibe. The long-vacant bank building is an exception. Its concrete block construction was purposeful as a safeguard against flooding. Concrete seemed like a smart move after three devastating flash floods over its 160-year history—in 1884, 1904, and 1956—destroyed the town. When the rain falls fast and hard here, the water has nowhere to go but down Bridge and Keyes creeks, through a narrow canyon and across Mitchell.

It could happen again anytime. Take April 2019, for example. Thunderstorms released nearly two inches of rain starting at 4:30 p.m. on a Friday. A river of mud, rocks, and debris rushed down steep hillsides and along Main Street only 30 minutes later. Landslides on the nearby hills forced the closure of Highway 26.

But when the sky is clear and the creek doesn't rise, which is most of the time, Mitchell is a popular tourist stop during what Shawn calls "mobile home season." The top attractions are the sprawling John Day Fossil Beds National Monument and specifically the Painted Hills Unit 10 miles west.

We find a table on the brewery's patio; the heat has subsided and it's pleasant this evening. With burgers and beers ordered, we lean back and relax. Our long, scorching day is over and we're already thinking about tomorrow. A group of firefighters sit at the next table and, like us, look as though they've had a tough day. They tell us there's a wildfire south of Mitchell and a base camp is assembling just west of town. We are reassured when these professionals say they don't expect flames or smoke will threaten our plans this week. We're riding away from the danger zone.

The wildfire threat is now commonplace and avoiding flames is only one of our concerns. We must check our weather and climate apps before traveling. A planned tour in Eastern Oregon last summer was canceled because smoke from a distant blaze created hazardous air quality. Drifting smoke also has on occasion obscured my view of the water at Crater Lake National Park.

Even our effort to ride all 17 scenic bikeways this year is in limbo. A fatal conflagration swept across the western slopes of the Cascades last September. As a result, the Cascading Rivers Scenic Bikeway from Estacada to Detroit remains closed while crews remove fallen trees and address safety concerns. There's no indication when those roads will reopen.

Like our extremely hot summer days, wildfires are a reality in Oregon. It's part of the new normal in our changing world climate.

There's one more stop this evening, a drive to the Painted Hills Overlook to see what the famous natural landmark looks like at sunset. As we turn from Highway 26 to narrow, winding Burnt Ranch Road, we see a small, distinctly colorful rise on our right. It's our first hint of what's to come. The road continues for another three or four miles until we reach the gravel Bear Creek Road, our final mile to the overlook. We are there a few minutes later.

A middle-aged couple, using the same paved trail we walk, take two or three photos with a mobile phone, walk 50 feet, and then stop to take more pictures as they search for the best angle to capture this geologic wonder. We do much the same thing, hoping to make one image that fully captures this enormous, beautiful sight.

These hills, stretching almost a mile long, were formed about 30 million years ago give or take 5 million years, geologists say. Periods of volcanic activity spread layers of ash, iron oxides, and other materials across the region. Then, as the earth changed over the hundreds of millennia, each layer took on differing hues. Wetter climates altered the color of the fresh deposits, enhancing red color bands 100 to 150 feet high. When the climate shifted to the dry side, the soil turned yellow. Earth's artistry left behind a distinctive sight for photographers, hikers, and we three cycling tourists to behold.

Oregon has been my home for 27 years yet this is the first time I've ever seen these hills. I stare, admire, and try to embrace the fact I'm looking at millions of years of change. An evening wind picks up, distracting me from the view and sweeping away the final thoughts of the day's experience. It's time to head back to the hostel.

Sam Blake, a paramedic from Asheville, N.C., looks weary and he has good reason to. Sam is riding across the TransAmerica Trail. He arrived at Spoke'n Hostel this afternoon and he'll be gone in the morning. We sit down in the hostel's common space and talk.

"Don't quote me as a cyclist," Sam says, as I activate my voice recorder. "I'm more like a professional idiot on a bike."

He details the trials and tribulations of riding a bicycle day after day across the continent, the changing landscape, hazards along the way, and his drive to complete the task. As we talk, my mind volleys the idea of such an undertaking. It's quickly dismissed; I have no desire to do anything of this sort yet I'm in awe of anyone who does.

Sam will leave Mitchell tomorrow heading west to Prineville, Sisters, the McKenzie Pass, and Coburg before turning north through the Willamette Valley. Once he arrives at the crossroads Polk County village of Rickreall, he veers west to the Pacific Ocean and up the coastline to Astoria, the trail's terminus.

I have questions, and Sam seems happy to answer.

Do you ever take detours from the official route and explore?

"I have had this debate the whole time about whether I want to deviate from the route," Sam says. "Obviously, at this point I'm committed but tomorrow I'm thinking about taking a day and heading to Bend. It's something different and I'm tired of riding past the really cool places by five or 10 miles. Yeah, that's not the right way to tour. This is my first tour and I'm going to do it differently next time for that reason."

Where will you reconnect with the route after you leave Bend?

"I connect back up in Sisters. It looks like that's the route I'll probably take."

And you'll go over McKenzie Pass?

"That will be cake. I think I'll probably knock off 100 miles that day. I'm conditioned for that climb. These grades are very rideable, in my opinion. The steep inclines of 7 and 8 percent don't compare to 15 and 20 in the Appalachians. It just doesn't. From day three, I walked at least three times a day, most of the time it was like 10 times a day, until I hit Kansas. That was the first time I could actually ride the whole day without walking. My bike's not built with that kind of gearing but there's nothing you can do but go forward."

Why did you decide to do this?

"Oh, gosh, I met some people a couple years ago in Europe that were touring. They bought bikes in Amsterdam, and I thought that it was a cool way to travel. I was interested in that, so I looked into it and came across this [trail]. It's been on my list for a couple years now."

The conversation continues for more than an hour as kindred spirits swap anecdotes from the road. We talk about bikes, challenges while riding, and his many run-ins with dogs chasing him down country roads. One even bit him but didn't draw blood. I ask how the expedition tested his resolve.

"Once you're in the middle of the hills, in the middle of nowhere, and you look around and there's no support and you're by yourself and it's up to you to get to the next place, the only thing to do is just either push on or give up, which is actually impossible when you're in the middle of nowhere," Sam says. "You just sort of suck it up and deal with it."

Well, that sounds like a credit to your perseverance.

"That's the term I would use to describe this trip. I don't think it's a physicality issue. I really don't. I can knock 100, 150 miles off physically right now. No problem. It's whether I want to deal with the 100-degree heat, the 110-degree heat a couple days ago, you know. My most vertical day was 6,300 feet. It's an issue of whether or not you want to push on. So, perseverance is how I would describe it."

It's a mental game, he says. There have been amazing moments and devastatingly mental, emotional breakdowns. "And that's where the perseverance comes in," Sam says, "whether or not you want to finish."

Mitchell – July 8, 2021

I'm up early and Sam is already gone, presumably pedaling toward Bend. Intent not to repeat yesterday's mistakes, Patti and Bob are awake and motivated as well. We gather our bags, bikes, and road food for the car. Breakfast is next (oatmeal, a muffin, and a banana for me) and we're ready to go. But first, we sign the guest book and leave cash donations to help support Jalet and Patrick in their good work.

Have I eaten enough for breakfast? Am I going to bonk halfway through my morning? I grab a cinnamon raisin bagel from our supplies and toast it to bring out the flavor. I eat half and wrap the rest in a paper towel. It slides into a back jersey pocket for a mid-morning road snack.

We're packed and ready to go by 7 a.m. There's a 10-mile prelude from Mitchell back to the Painted Hills. We drove this way last night to see the hills at sunset but now we return to make sure we complete this extension of the bikeway's southernmost tentacle by bike. But time is precious; another hot day is forecast. Sam may not be the only idiot on a bike today, but we will persevere. Patti and I pedal out while Bob drives to the gravel turnoff near the Painted Hills and leaves the car before riding back toward Mitchell. We meet along the way, pausing for a group selfie.

With the opening segment completed, we head to Route 26 Espresso, a drive-through coffee stand on the edge of town. Bob arrives moments later. We're drinking our usuals: doppio macchiatos. These are not the Starbucks-variant but the true Italian macchiato—two shots of espresso and a touch of foamed half-and-half. Most baristas I encounter know nothing of this concoction, assuming 20-some ounces of milk, sugar, syrup, and a little coffee is the real thing. No matter where we stop, we order by description and not proper name.

Call us snobs. I can accept that. Bob speaks passable Italian and I know a little, much less than Bob. We know the word *macchiato* means stained. Two shots of espresso stained with half-and-half works well for us.

I walk up to the Route 26 Espresso window and place the order. "Two shots of espresso, please, with a little half-and-half," I say to the man inside. With drinks in hand, we sit by a small gazebo enjoying the moment before getting back on the bikes. The coffees are exceptional, we decide, and I return to the window to compliment the barista.

While appreciative, he didn't seem surprised. Compliments flow like caffeine at Route 26 Espresso where bicyclists, often as discerning about their coffee as they are their bikes, stop, drink, and tip the barista.

"We get about 2,500 bicyclists a year coming through Mitchell," says Steve Tripp, Route 26's owner, barista, and town mayor. "We've had people riding bikes coming through here from all over the world. We do get compliments on our coffee. It's not bitter. We like the taste and texture."

Caffeine infused, we drive to the junction of Twickenham Road and Highway 207. There are 50 more miles ahead to finish the Painted Hills bikeway. Before starting, we invent and immediately invoke the Bob Rule. Here it is: If there's an extremely difficult hill ahead, Bob does it. Sure, Patti and I have the option to join him, but the reality is that Bob craves riding the hard grades at speeds faster than our capabilities. We would only slow him down. We're doing him a favor.

Patti and I start from the junction and ride 14 miles north to Service Creek, where highways 207 and 19 meet. There's a general store and a small lodge here. This is a good place for lunch, we agree, but it's still early and Bob has a hill to climb. He takes his steel-frame Torelli from the back of the car; Patti and I strap our bikes on the rack. Bob is going to ride nine miles up to Butte Creek Pass while Patti and I drive ahead and leave the car at the top for him. Then we'll glide those same nine miles back down and have lunch. Perhaps honored by a new rule bearing his name, Bob embraces the task. He always does.

A sign a mile from the top points to Julia Henderson Pioneer Park, 40 acres of land that has served as a campground, wedding venue, and the place for countless community socials for more than a century. A historical marker credits Julia for donating the land to the community in 1900. Little else is explained. I want to know more.

Research reveals she was born Julia Ann Baird in December 1840 or sometime in 1841 in Tippecanoe County, Indiana, and moved west with her family 12 years later, perhaps over the Oregon Trail as countless others did in the mass migration. She married Ira Albert Henderson in 1858 in Brownsville and the couple lived on 160 acres there and later in Heppner before finally settling in Fossil where they lived for many years. An 1870 census document listed Ira as a "stockdealer" and Julia's occupation as "keeping house." It also shows they had four young children at the time.

An obituary prepared for a Fossil newspaper following Ira's death described him as having strong ethics and morals. He was a church steward, a Mason, and an active member of the Fossil community. The land dedicated in Julia's name was donated 17 years before Ira died in 1917. Julia passed away in 1928.

There's no picture of Julia. The park gate is closed and locked. We move on.

Patti and I begin our descent, first past Rowe Creek Road where boiling asphalt almost finished me yesterday, past Julia's park one more time, and past Bob who is still pedaling his way up. I firmly grip the brakes to control my speed; the bike computer mounted on my handlebar reads 35.8 mph.

There's little traffic; the road is ours. I love the Bob Rule.

We arrive back in Service Creek. Only my hands are tired from squeezing the brakes. We have lunch at a picnic table; I'll take a grilled cheese sandwich for the much-needed protein and calories. Then we're off again following the John Day River for 25 very hot miles, through the town of Spray and on to the bikeway junction of Kimberly where the Painted Hills and Old West routes meet. We stop under the shade of a row of oak trees knowing we met our goal for the day. We'll be back here tomorrow.

Professional idiots, indeed.

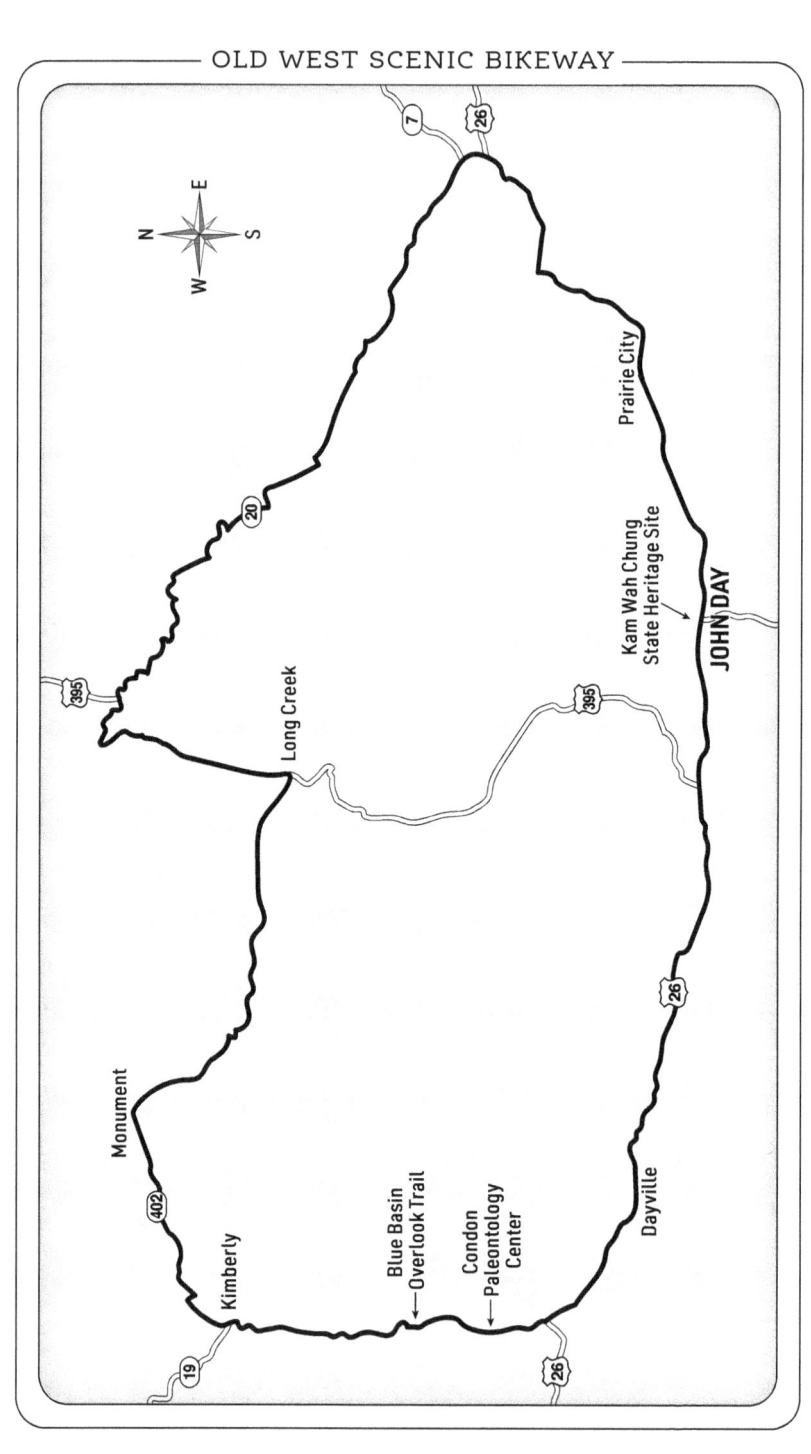

Horses. Cats. Canines. Turtles.
Old West Scenic Bikeway

• • •

Start and Finish: John Day
Distance: 174 miles
Elevation Gain: 8,493 feet
Rating: Challenging

Dayville – July 9, 2021

We're patching together today's segments in an unorthodox manner. The Old West Scenic Bikeway starts and ends in John Day, according to the official map, but we're following a different progression. We have three days to complete this 174-mile loop and we want to finish in Kimberly, a point from which we can easily navigate to Interstate 84, Portland, and home. Lodging is non-existent in Kimberly, so we spent last night in Dayville 25 miles down the road.

Once fueled by fresh coffee and egg burritos from Twisted Treasures and Gnarly Goods in Dayville, we start the bicycle ride north back to Kimberly. Burritos would not have been our first choice, but food options are limited at 6:30 a.m. here and Twisted Treasures is convenient. No complaints. The food is good and the coffee is strong.

The cool, fresh morning air is a relief after two days of intense heat. It's actually chilly once the pedaling starts and air flashes across bare legs. We follow quiet Highway 26 along the John Day River until we see a line of hills ahead. There's a thin gap that looks as if an earthquake of immeasurable magnitude fractured and then separated the earth. Once we enter the gap, we discover the river is following along the same path. Geologists report 17 lava flows covered this area beginning about 16 million years ago. The river then began carving its way through the residual basalt rock leaving this short yet deep gorge. Native peoples later created rock imagery on nearby canyon walls prompting the modern name Picture Gorge. These images, etched and painted, were created thousands of years ago. Artists are unknown.

"At some point water started carving at it, cutting down that particular gorge to get to where it is," says Nick Famoso, a National Parks Service ranger and head paleontologist at the John Day Fossil Beds National Monument. "This is fairly shallow compared to the Columbia Gorge. That stuff was deposited at the same time as this but, obviously, the John Day River is not the Columbia River."

The John Day River looks more like a stream here. It doesn't get larger until it reaches Kimberly, Nick says, and even then it's never comparable to the Columbia. Still, Picture Gorge is stunning to see. Our heads swivel as the road curls around rock faces, looking left and right at the rugged, layered hillsides on both sides.

We emerge on the north side and make our way toward Blue Basin, Cathedral Rock, and the Thomas Condon Paleontology Center, the national monument's interpretive museum. This is the place to get a clear understanding of what the John Day Fossil Beds National Monument represents and what is found in its three distinct units, Clarno, Painted Hills, and Sheep Rock. This also is where Nick and his team process and display fossils discovered during meticulous field research.

The center is named for Thomas Condon, a congregationalist minister and self-trained paleontologist who found fossils in this region. Condon first started exploring the area in 1865 and eventually sent his findings to East Coast scholars for verification. Some of his work made its way to the Smithsonian Institution and earned him a position in 1872 as the first Oregon State Geologist. He became the first professor of Natural History at the University of Oregon and continued to teach there until he died in 1907.

We take a right turn a few miles north of the interpretive center and pedal up a short, steep driveway-like road. At the top is a small parking lot, the starting point for the 1.3-mile Island in Time loop trail. A walking path leads into Blue Basin and a 360-degree view of the Turtle Cove Member of the John Day Formation, exposed stratified hillsides that draw linear definition to millions of years of change. Stand on the trail and see geologic history in the round.

"There are at least 100 known fossil animal species here," Nick says, explaining that the bottom of the rock layer is about 31 million years old and the top, the more recent strata, dates back only 27 or 28 million years. "So, we're not talking about a huge amount of time, geologically speaking, and there's a very large diversity of animals that were living in this area at the time."

The John Day Fossil Beds National Monument, at about 14,000 acres in size, is representative of what paleontologists can find in various parts of Central and Eastern Oregon, he says. These fossils reflect changes in climate, habitat, and the species that lived and died here. Horses. Cats. Canines. Turtles. But don't expect to find one bed of bones. Small bits of evidence are scattered through the sedimentary rocks and across the millions of millennia if you know where and how to look.

"That's what most people expect when they come here," Nick says. "They're like 'oh, where are the fossil beds?' And what they really mean is, 'is there a bone bed somewhere?' The answer is no. But we do produce a ton of fossils. There's stuff that we find every year, new fossils that are being discovered."

The Clarno, Sheep Rock, and Painted Hills units were incorporated into one entity when Congress established the monument in 1975. This, Nick says, is the longest record of evolution preserved in one place covering about 50 million years. "And there's really nowhere else like this in the [National] Park Service, probably in the country, that produces that much in one spot," Nick says. "And that's part of the reason why we were able to set it aside as a national monument.

"And, look at all these flood deposits that you can see are then held up by these ash layers. You can see that repetitiveness—layer, layer, layer, layer, layer, layer—and that's just how volcanically active this region was."

Away from the parking lot and down the short hill, we turn north and reset our sights on Kimberly. We still have one more landmark before we get there. I know Cathedral Rock is three miles ahead and, sensing a photo opportunity, I pedal ahead of Bob to find a turnout and a good photo angle. Bob slows his pace to give me a head start. I reach Cathedral Rock's towering wall and it looks much like Blue Basin. Layer, layer, layer, layer,

layer, layer. There's also a horizontal stripe more than halfway up, as there was at Blue Basin, that shines almost aquamarine due to the mineral celadonite in the clay.

I look for my spot knowing Bob soon will appear from around the bend. I want to take a picture as he passes in front of the wall. I hurry, not wanting to miss the moment, and then I wait in silence.

I haven't seen a vehicle for nearly an hour. This is solitude. A light breeze arrives, ruffling the leaves above and behind me. A lone bird peeps as if to say I am not alone. This is the bird's domain, and I am a visitor. I wonder who else over the centuries stopped here and listened to the birds. Did native peoples fish this bank of the John Day River only 100 feet in front of me?

This is why we ride. We're far from big cities, miles from any town. Is there any reason why I should be standing here early on a summer morning? I'm here because the bicycle allows me to be. I forget for a moment why I'm here, only knowing that I am. A new sound is heard, a blended whirl that is easily recognized as a bike chain turning gears and wheels rolling on asphalt. I look to see Bob easing around the bend, approaching my photo field. I am ready. The phone camera is up. Click-click-click. I capture as many frames as possible before he passes by. I check the screen for results. Success.

Perhaps a quarter-mile down the road, I think back to that moment. The wind. The bird. The sound of the river water flowing nearby. I don't have a notepad to write this down, so I commit it all to memory. It's a really good memory.

We arrive in Kimberly just as we did yesterday only from the opposite direction. This is a T-intersection, not a town, but there is a general store. Two old, abandoned buildings stand across the road. One could have been a storefront at one time while the adjacent building perhaps was a storage unit. The wood on each now looks dark, weathered, and rough-hewn. They lean as if waiting for a strong gust of wind to bring them down.

There's a road sign showing we're at a rare junction where two scenic bikeways meet. I look west to see where we came in yesterday afternoon and I look southeast and see what we just accomplished. To the north is Long Creek Highway, our route when we return here a final time in two days.

There are three names to know in Grant County.

Let's start with a man named John Day. Lacking much documentation, historians have pieced together an account of a hunter and trapper from Virginia who came to the Oregon territory in 1812 as what the Oregon Historical Society website calls "a straggler" from the Pacific Fur Company expedition to Astoria.

Washington Irving, the American writer best remembered for his short stories *Rip Van Winkle* and *The Legend of Sleepy Hollow,* published a two-volume book in 1836 about John Jacob Astor's Pacific Fur Company titled *Astoria: or Anecdotes of an Enterprise Beyond the Rocky Mountains.* In it, based on research and journals from those who were there, Irving describes John Day as 40 years old and perhaps 6 feet, 2 inches tall with a "handsome, open, manly countenance." He was "a prime woodsman, and an almost unerring shot" with "an elastic step as if he trod on springs."

Other accounts tell how Day became ill on the way to the Pacific Ocean. Some say Day fell victim to "excesses" and his illness was a result of his unspecified indulgences. He was left behind with another man, Ramsey Crooks, according to accounts, as the expedition moved on. The pair continued at their own pace until a group of native men confronted them where a river flowed into the Columbia. Seeking justice for a tribal member's death, the group took the two men's weapons and left them naked to fend for themselves. A few days later, another group from the fur company found the men along the same river. In time, that water became known as the John Day River.

This ignominious event led to future naming rights for the cities of John Day and Dayville, the John Day Fossil Beds National Monument, and other geographic locations, structures, and organizations.

We roll into the city bearing his name by mid-afternoon and after some prerequisite recovery time, Patti and I decide to explore this community of 1,600. John Day, we learn, was a mining town about 160 years ago after gold was discovered near Whiskey Flat about four miles down the road. Local legend has it more than 1,000 men were camping along Canyon Creek within 10 days after the discovery. About $26 million in gold was reportedly pulled over time from deposits there and near Susanville 35 miles north, and as a result Eastern Oregon enjoyed an economic boom until the veins tapped out.

A quarter mile from our Dreamers Lodge motel is the Kam Wah Chung State Heritage Site Interpretive Center, a small, white, one-story building that illustrates the story of the area's two other prominent historical figures, Lung On and Ing "Doc" Hay. While John Day seemingly left his name without much more than a passing connection with the region, Lung On and Ing Hay lived their adult lives here and made lasting impressions on the local community as well as Oregon's Chinese history. Walk two more minutes down the street and stand outside the Kam Wah Chung building, an odd structure with stone walls supporting the ground floor and a sturdy, exterior wooden staircase leading up to a wood-framed second story. This building is the epicenter of an archeological, cultural, and historical treasure trove.

Chinese immigrants hoping to find work in the gold mines rushed to this area in the late 19th century despite strong racial hostility. They made their way to Canyon City and a self-supporting community took shape. Fires would repeatedly destroy their enclave, yet the immigrants would rebuild each time until 1885 when white Canyon City lawmakers outlawed another reconstruction. About 400 people packed what they had left and moved two miles to John Day's existing Chinese community.

Isolated due to racist norms of the era, Chinese residents had to fend for themselves. Seeing an opportunity, Lung On and Ing Hay in 1888 purchased a 17-year-old Kam Wah Chung and Co. building, a location that possibly was once a stagecoach stop or trading post. They opened for business with Lung On as an entrepreneur and merchant store owner and Ing Hay as a healer operating an apothecary. Kam Wah Chung quickly became a commercial and cultural center, eventually serving John Day's Chinese and white communities. Kam Wah Chung was a doctor's office, a pharmacy, a general store, a boarding house, an unofficial post office, and a religious center.

"That is right at the height of the Chinese Exclusion Act so except for merchants, for the most part, Chinese were not allowed to own property. They were not allowed to do banking, they were not allowed to do a lot of things," says Don Merritt, museum curator at the Kam Wah Chung State Heritage Site, part of the Oregon State Parks system. "Well, these two gentlemen, particularly Lung On because he could read and write English very well, were able to communicate with the Chinese and non-Chinese. Lung On would help people write letters home. He would help with legal matters. He would help with businesses. He really was the linchpin that held the two communities together."

And while Lung On was taking care of business, Ing Hay was quickly earning his nickname as "Doc." "He was able to treat a lot of the Chinese and once the Chinese left by 1910, he transitioned over to help the non-Chinese," Don says. "A lot of patients are coming to him. We have numerous examples of this."

While official numbers placed John Day's Chinese population at about 1,000, Don says the actual total could have been as high as 2,000. People would live in town during the winter and then return to nearby gold camps when the weather improved. Still, most immigrants used Kam Wah Chung as their mailing address.

And business was good until Lung On died in December 1940. Doc Hay continued with the apothecary until 1948 when he broke a hip and was moved to Portland for convalescence. No one realized it at the time, but the business entity Kam Wah Chung was closed forever.

"Doc Hay thought he'd be back in a few weeks," Don says. "He just locked the doors and windows and left. Eventually, he had to be put into a nursing home because of medical complications and other factors. He was expecting to come back, but he never did."

When the doors were reopened 20 years later, everything was found exactly as Doc Hay had left it. And it all remains the same today. "Oh yeah, absolutely, everything is still there pretty much as it was left," Don says.

It's all there; the medicines, the canned goods, the paperwork, the mortar and pestle for mixing medicines, cans of Prince Albert tobacco, a cast iron stove, pots and pans on wall hooks, even a faded calendar on the wall. Nearly 20,000 artifacts were found. In all, Kam Wah Chung made up what visiting Chinese scholars would later call the world's largest intact collection of Chinese medicines and documentation.

The account of Lung On's and Ing Hay's Kam Wah Chung is told in both the museum building and small interpretive center. Progress is being made on a new $4.5 million facility that will be constructed adjacent to the old building, a place where John Day's Chinatown stood for decades. The new center, tentatively scheduled to open in 2027, will take some stress off the old building, Don says. "Every time we go in there, a little piece of it deteriorates because people are breathing inside it and affecting the artifacts."

John Day – July 10, 2021

I avoid major highways and busy roads when I ride. When cycling near traffic, I look for extra-wide road shoulders. Safety is Priority No. 1 but I don't feel safe today.

We leave John Day before 8 a.m., once again to avoid the heat. Unfortunately, we can't escape the trucks on Highway 26. All my safety rules are tossed aside as Patti and I start east. We have one lane in each direction and limited shoulders. There's no alternative route and we have 13 miles between us and the next town, Prairie City.

That equates to nearly an hour with eyes constantly looking

into rear-view mirrors watching for the morning sun reflecting off chrome as fast-moving semi-trailer trucks bear down on us at speeds in excess of 60 mph.

Patti and I don't talk about it, but we both know the peril and we're pedaling at a fast pace. To our advantage, there's little wind and the narrower-than-desired shoulder is in decent condition. A road crew recently resurfaced the highway here and while traffic lanes are bumpy with heavy chip seal, the shoulders have not been touched, leaving a much smoother surface. This is the way it should be done, says Patti, a retired ODOT employee.

We are racing against distance, time, and danger. Bob, meanwhile, is driving to Prairie City where he will leave the car and start uphill on his own where road conditions are safer. Once Patti and I arrive there, I will assume the driving and Patti will follow after Bob. We will rendezvous at the Austin House, a roadside diner 15 miles up the road.

I watch the daily mileage total click up on my bike GPS display. The risk of getting clipped by a mass of steel barreling toward us is reduced with each tenth of a mile. We have our taillights blinking as warning and we wear bright, reflective jackets with the hope the colors will be noticed. Mine is yellow, Patti's is bright pink. We can tell if a truck driver sees us; the vehicle appears in the mirror as it gradually angles left over the center yellow line, straddling the middle of the road and adding distance between its right, front fender and our back wheels. We're buffeted by its turbulence once it passes.

I lose count. Eight, maybe 10 big trucks pass us as well as a small collection of speeding pickup trucks. They all take a wide berth, respecting Oregon's safe passing law which states that a vehicle passing a bicyclist while traveling 35 mph or faster must provide enough space to avoid contact were the bicyclist to fall over into the lane of traffic. Many Oregon motorists don't know this law exists, but every driver passing us today abides by its intent.

We arrive in Prairie City unscathed if not unnerved. I look for fresh coffee in this small downtown, but no stores are open. It's not yet 9 a.m. We grab our water bottles and sit down at a picnic table outside the town's public works building, a single-story brick structure with a western-style wood façade facing Front Street, Prairie City's main thoroughfare. A mural stretches across the brick building's west wall. To the right is a large cityscape circa 2001, the year local art teacher Toni Morgensen painted it. To the left are four windows, each painted as though they actually open to offices inside. Children and adults appear in the portals, their dress suggesting we're seeing how the old building and its occupants would have appeared a century earlier. This is one of two murals the schoolteacher created, both greeting travelers as they enter Prairie City from either side of town. A "Welcome to Prairie City" mural painted a year later adorns the side of the historic Hotel Prairie and honors the role of the steam locomotive in Grant County's development.

We take a short walk about town in a final, futile attempt to find coffee before Patti resumes her ride. She still needs to climb nine miles and 1,792 feet up and over the Dixie Pass Summit (elevation 5,277 feet) before dropping 1,000 feet to the Austin House. Once there, we find our coveted coffee and oversized pastries, perfect fuel for our next segment, Grant County Road 20.

I've been looking forward to this. Maps show a squiggly white line for 40 miles alongside the Middle Fork of the John

Day River from Bates State Park northwest to Highway 395. Now I see that the white line is narrow, remote pavement twisting around bend after bend as it follows the course of the river.

I am on the lookout for one creature—rattlesnakes. Tammy Bremner, office manager at the Grant County Chamber of Commerce, warned me weeks ago that rattlers like to slither from the grass onto the pavement and warm themselves. Keep an eye out, she said. I wasn't concerned at the time and I'm not now though I can't say how I'll react if I see one. Let's hope the snake is near the side of the road and I'm on the center line.

There are other encounters along this road. There's a 21st century cowboy on horseback guiding 11 cattle that don't notice when our car, a relatively quiet Toyota Highlander hybrid, slowly rolls up from behind. The car is moving on electric power with little more noise than rubber tires rolling on asphalt. The moms and calves eventually see the car but don't seem concerned; they decide to trot alongside instead of veering away in fear.

We've passed stray cows and bulls throughout our four days in Wheeler and Grant counties. I'm more concerned about the possibility of their sudden moves than they seem to be of mine. For years I've seen videos of large animals lunging at, rushing toward, or knocking over unsuspecting cyclists. I want no part of that.

Cattle are not our only sightings on Road 20. We count two dogs, three deer, one coyote, two cyclists on e-bikes, six cars and trucks, and two dead adolescent rattlesnakes during this three-hour stretch. It appears the snakes ventured too close to the center line.

The road continues rolling on a slight downhill grade with the river as a near constant companion, and we approach the town of Galena after about 20 miles. We've been told this is a ghost town, a remnant of the 1860s gold rush era. Small, dilapidated and abandoned buildings are collapsing on themselves. Roofs have fallen within the remaining exterior walls and weeds have taken up residence.

But if Galena were a ghost town, the spirits would be very busy. A general store on the right side of the roadway has been restored. Another structure has been rebuilt as a small church. There's also a jail and a bank, each created to look as if they dated back to the gold rush. They still look weathered but are topped with bright, new roofs.

The town was originally settled near the confluence of the Middle Fork and Elk Creek as a mining community, according to local records. Originally named Susanville after an early inhabitant, Susan Ward, the town moved two miles north in 1900 or 1901 when a post office was established. The location took a new name, Galena, after the lead sulfide commonly found in Oregon's gold and copper veins.

We quickly pass Galena and push on toward Highway 395. This is our stopping point for the day, as we decided this morning, and my anticipation grows with each mile. I'm tired and ready to end this for the day. Bob and Patti finish ahead of me by several minutes and, once back together, they announce they are rested and ready to go again. On the other hand, I only see the road tilting up. Wanting no part of another climb today, I gladly agree to take a turn driving 13 miles to our Long Creek motel.

The paper map profile indicates there is a steady climb for almost four miles and then a relaxing downhill glide to town. Bob charges up the grade while Patti methodically turns the pedals at her own pace. I drive to the crest and discover that the downhill slope we expected is actually a series of big, undulating rollers that eventually finish down at Long Creek. Bob and Patti won't get there without a lot of effort.

Patti shakes her head bewildered or disappointed, I don't ask which, when I return and share the news. She perseveres, finally cresting her last hill and easing into Long Creek, but her tired expression reveals the toll of another long day on the bike. We left John Day more than eight hours and 82 miles ago. She approaches the center of this tiny town, turns right and then quickly angles left into the parking lot of the Long Creek Lodge.

The pain is quickly forgotten as talk turns to food. There aren't many choices in Long Creek. There's a food cart, the Chuckwagon with burgers and sandwiches, right next to the motel. Our other option is to walk to the other side of the intersection and the Long Creek General Store and Café. The deciding factor? Seating at the food cart is limited to a picnic table under a still-warm sun. We prefer the café's air conditioning.

Long Creek – July 11, 2021

We wake knowing we'll be home tonight. It's only 35 miles to Kimberly, an easy spin to finish our tour along the Old West Scenic Bikeway. Patti and I leave Long Creek and ride west on Highway 402. It's crisp, almost cold at 6:30 a.m. Our sight lines stretch in all directions across gently rolling terrain to the distant horizon. We see some hills far ahead, but they don't concern us. We know this will be an easy day. There's no concern over 35 miles with only 1,000 feet of climbing.

Rather than shuttle the car, Bob drives all the way to Kimberly and reverses his ride toward us. Patti and I, meanwhile, continue at our leisurely pace. We stop to take pictures, we watch the landscape change from open range to basalt outcrops spotted with juniper trees, we savor the downhills and speed through Hamilton, a community of three houses. Accounts indicate the town was named after J.H. Hamilton, a rancher who settled here in 1874. By 1993, only three residences remained. Outbuildings long abandoned and deteriorating serve as decaying reminders of Hamilton's ranching era.

We stop at a turnout about 25 miles into our day to study a roadside information plate fastened to a small boulder. The placard explains the "Geology of Long Creek Mountain and Round Basin," reminding us once more that Oregon is primarily a volcanic lava flow on top of previous lava flows. The plate instructs us to spot natural landmarks in the distance in order to follow the Hamilton fault line. More study reveals how the fault pushed the Picture Gorge basalt formation 800 feet. Patti sees it first, then helps guide my eye. There it is.

Moving again, it's only minutes before Bob approaches from the other direction. We exchange waves as we would do with any stranger passing on a bike. Bob is on a determined ride uphill; no time for chitchat. For Patti and me, it's all downhill from here. We enter Monument, population 128, looking for a cold drink at Boyer's Store. Passing a church, we hear singing from inside. The store is closed. It's Sunday morning. We reverse course one block and return to Highway 402, the Long Creek Highway, where we wave to a woman weeding in her front yard. She's the only person we see in Monument.

Only 14 comfortable miles remain to Kimberly. Bob has turned around and is headed back to the car. We arrive about 10 minutes before him, just enough time to peruse the ice cream selections inside the John Day River Trading Post. First to greet us is Nessie, a large red creature, half Bernese Mountain Dog and the other half a mix of St. Bernard and Mastiff. Nessie lumbers toward us, perhaps to say hello or perhaps to help pick out our ice cream.

Kayla Hand appears from the backroom moments later. Kayla, who owns the store with her sister, grew up in Kimberly and moved back several years ago to be near family. The sisters reopened the store in 2014, which Kayla says has stood on this corner for decades, referring to a 1926 photo as evidence. "I grew up about four miles down the road," she says. "I used to ride my bike here when I was a kid."

I ask why she came back.

"I like the rural area. For us, this is home," she says. "You don't find a place more beautiful than Kimberly with the fossil beds and all the geology. It's one of the last remote places. I like being out in the middle of nowhere. It suits me well. We don't even have cell phone service."

Do you see many cyclists here?

"We get a lot of bicyclists. We get international travelers and bicycle tours. We even had a race come through here."

What do cyclists buy in your store?

Dried apples harvested from the nearby orchard, she says. Chocolate milk. "And, ice cream, of course."

Patti and Bob eventually settle onto a large, rocking wooden bench in front of the store. I clickity click across the road, the metal clips on the bottoms of my bike shoes tapping as I step, and stare at a street sign indicating the intersection of the Painted Hills and Old West scenic bikeways. We've been here twice before this week, and I don't know when I'll be back again. I'm happy to be here now.

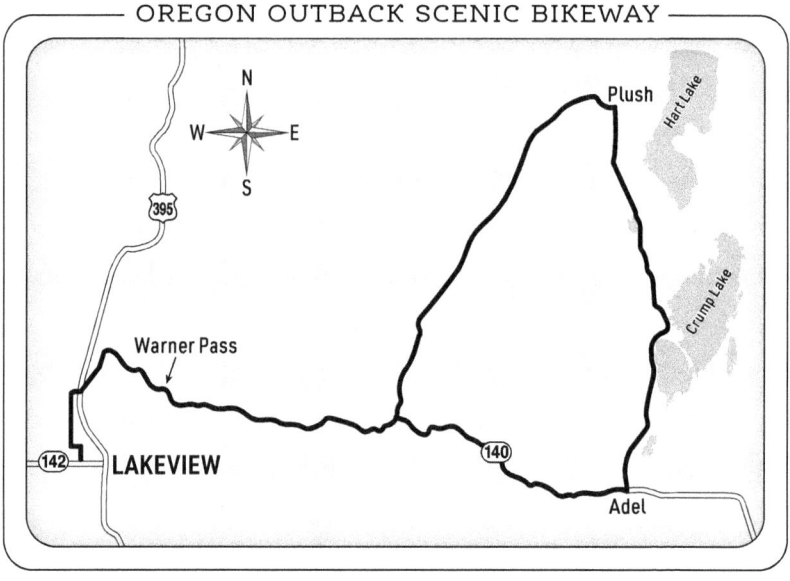

OREGON OUTBACK SCENIC BIKEWAY

11

'There's More Cows Per Square Mile Than People'

Oregon Outback Scenic Bikeway

• • •

Start and Finish: Lakeview
Distance: 89 miles
Elevation Gain: 4,327 feet
Rating: Extreme

Lakeview – July 26, 2021

The downtown streets are quiet on a weekday morning and that comes as no surprise to Thom Batty, owner of Tall Town Bike & Camp. There are only 2,600 Lakeview city residents and about 7,000 people in the Lake County. "There's more cows per square mile than people," Thom says. "I'm sure you probably noticed."

At 4,800 feet elevation, Lakeview brands itself the "Tallest Town in Oregon." Thom calls this his adopted home, a unique territory he discovered on a reconnaissance trip. Thom operated a bicycle tour concierge service in metro Portland several years ago and came here in search of new tour destinations. "I came through town and fell in love with the place. There's a huge recreational opportunity here."

Thom is taking advantage of it. His store caters to mountain as well as road bicyclists, hikers, snow skiers, campers, and even stargazers. There's so little light pollution here at night that Lake County is renowned for having some of the darkest skies in America. The nearby community of Plush records zero light pollution and it's so dark atop Hart Mountain that you can see the Milky Way, Thom says.

Mountain biking captures the headlines in Lake County. The 669-mile Oregon Timber Trail bikepacking route along the Cascade Range goes through here. "We've had people from pretty much all over the world coming here to ride [the Timber Trail]," he says. "I've had riders stop in from Japan, Scotland, the Czech Republic, New Zealand."

I wonder how someone living in a fast-paced metro area would adjust to the slow, easy speed of a small ranching town. "Yeah, it's a culture shock," he concedes without regret. "It's small, and the weather is what I consider to be much more pleasant than the Portland area. It doesn't get scorching, scorching hot and, as they say, it's dry heat."

Lakeview is 95 miles east of Klamath Falls and less than 15 miles from the California border. There's no shortcut to get here; we angled southeast from the Willamette Valley via Eugene, Oakridge, Chemult, and Klamath Falls. Along on the trip are Bob, Patti, Eric, Robert Mansolillo and Mischa O'Reilly. Mischa is on the injured list after breaking her arm in a mountain bike accident, so she's our SAG [support and gear] driver. Having her behind the wheel helps us arrange a complicated car-bike ballet.

The Oregon Outback bikeway extends for 89 miles east of Lakeview and we have one day to ride it. This route is what I call a lasso route; Patti calls it a lollipop. There's an out-and-back section and a loop on one end. In this case, the rope or lollipop stick is 21 miles from Lakeview east, up and over the Warner Pass (5,845 feet), and past cattle ranches along the Warner Highway, State Route 140. The loop or candy starts when riders veer left to Plush Cutoff Road. This is 18 miles of high desert asphalt with sweeping views north and east. There's a lot of sagebrush and juniper here and not much else.

Instead of us all covering the entire distance, we each pick segments we want to ride with Mischa shuttling us from one place to another. This plan works for me. I rode 68 miles here last year, and today's logistics allow me to ride my favorite segments one more time and then finish the final 21 miles along the straight rope back to town.

I was alone with my thoughts riding this road in 2020. I recall no more than five trucks or RVs passing me on Plush Cutoff Road and I had little reason to stop for 75 minutes. That is until I heard an unusual crackling, hissing noise, a sound I'd never heard before. I rolled to a stop and stood straddling the bike frame. I reached forward and back, squeezing tires to check for air. This didn't sound like a tire problem, but it's typically my first move. No flats. I then realized I still heard the noise and I wasn't even moving. I looked up and discovered I was beneath high-voltage power lines. The noise was emanating from the wires.

The noise was the result of corona discharge. Under certain conditions, an electric field near energized components and conductors can create this discharge, and it is a common occurrence with higher voltage lines. In short, the noise was energy.

Back on my bike with that hissing sound fading behind me, I continued north to my designated meeting location with my wife Carla, a gravel lot just outside the community of Plush. Now, a year later, Mischa takes Patti and me to the same lot. We're heading south on Hogback Road toward Adel. Hogback Road passes south of Hart Mountain and near Hart and Crump lakes. The undulating road leaves us plenty of time to look east across the water to jutting hills on the other side. This is part of the Basin and Range region created millions of years ago, and we're riding where Ice Age glaciers once existed. Hart and Crump lakes were formed by the glaciers.

We coast down a final three-quarter mile and into a parking lot outside the Adel Store, a white, two-story, wood-frame building and gas station 30 miles east of Lakeview. An American flag gently waves atop its white flagpole. Mischa is here, leaning against the front of the car as Patti and I approach. There's a school, a church, and a post office in Adel. That's it.

Patti and I walk inside the store to fill our bottles with cold water, passing a kitchen on the right and turning into the small dining room. Four men sit at one table, clutching coffee cups. This appears to be a community hub for area ranchers. The four pause to look at this Lycra-wearing pair clicking their shoes on the floor, then quickly return to their conversation. They've seen our kind before, cook-server-cashier Stacey Martin tells us.

Our eyes focus on more than a dozen deer and elk heads, some with broad antlers, hanging on the walls. Horse saddles dangle suspended from the ceiling. We find bottled water in the refrigerated cabinet and head to Stacey at the cash register.

Back in the parking lot, we grab road provisions from the back of Mischa's hatchback. Bob, Eric, and Robert arrived while we were inside with the elk heads. Being the slowest of the riders, Patti and I get a head start for the return to Lakeview. We have 34 miles ahead of us, 12 back to the Plush Cutoff along Gibson Canyon and the final 21 over Warner Pass and down into Lakeview. We climb as Highway 140 follows the canyon and Deep Creek, then eventually Drake and Parsnip creeks. I tell Patti that we'll see Deep Creek Falls on our left, a 25-foot waterfall I first saw when I rode through here last year. It's not the same this time. We eventually see the falls, but there's no rushing sound and merely a trickle of water flowing down. Another victim of climate change and drought.

We continue until we reach a state highway crew and a flagger allowing cars and trucks through the area one direction at a time. This is our second road crew encounter today; the first was in Adel. A pilot vehicle pulls ahead of us and leads the way. Cars and trucks quickly follow the pilot leaving us behind at 14 mph. We now have the road to ourselves for a while. There's no oncoming traffic until we clear the construction area. We listen as a gentle wind brushes over the roadside vegetation. Birds chirp nearby.

I suddenly sense an object looming about 10 feet above me. It silently approaches from behind, off my left shoulder, and smoothly glides over me and ahead of my moving bike. I see for the first time it's a bald eagle—white head, dark brown body, and white, splayed tail feathers—with its majestic, full 6-foot wingspan casting a shadow on the ground. With another sudden aerial maneuver, it veers hard right, adjusts, and then left to fly parallel with me, still up about 10 feet and now ahead by 20. I'm mesmerized. This bird shows no outward concern for our presence, perhaps it welcomes company and wishes to join us if only for a moment. The eagle flying against a blue sky is at home in the wilderness; we are visitors along its path. Then, just as quickly, the eagle goes in a different direction. We pedal on.

Eric, Robert, and Bob catch us and we all meet Mischa at the Plush Cutoff junction for water and food. Mischa encourages us for those final miles. I'm feeling stronger than I anticipated, and eventually reach the Warner Pass summit with only modest fatigue. A lone cyclist appears moments later. Based on his fit physical appearance and enthusiasm, it's clear he's a local resident who spends a lot of time on his bike. He suggests we try secluded backroads and challenging hill climbs until we explain we're on a direct path back to town.

I'm first to go but Patti quickly blasts by me as she usually does. Then Bob. Then Eric. Then Robert. Then the local blurs past all of us, leaning forward from his seat, crouched low against his bicycle frame. He holds the handlebar in the center, not near the brakes, and his chin is only inches above his hands in a tight, tucked aerodynamic position. This is the absence of fear. If he were to ride over a small rock, he could tumble downhill at nearly 50 mph. But this is his road; it's clear he's done this many times before. He has faith in himself and his bike. He disappears in the distance.

(12)

'If You Really Want to Do Something, You Can Do It'

Cascade Siskiyou Scenic Bikeway

• • •

Start and Finish: Ashland
Distance: 55 miles
Elevation Gain: 5,085 feet
Rating: Extreme

Ashland – July 28, 2021

I can't look at my speedometer. I know my descent is fast, in all probability too fast. The wind blasting against my face slips around the curved edges of my sunglasses, moistening the corners of my eyes. The airflow snaps at my cycling jersey. The road is rough and rocky because the Jackson County Roads department is in the middle of a resurfacing project. The aggregate rock is laid down but the asphalt is still to come. Unfortunate timing on our part.

Unsure of the surface, I try to maintain a safe speed. Bob, Eric, Jennifer, and I followed this same Dead Indian Memorial Road in 2019 and I know it's very easy to go extremely fast here. I reached a nervous 41 mph then, but I have no intention of doing the same this time.

Still, the adrenalin-pumped thrill of speed is counterbalanced

CASCADE SISKIYOU SCENIC BIKEWAY

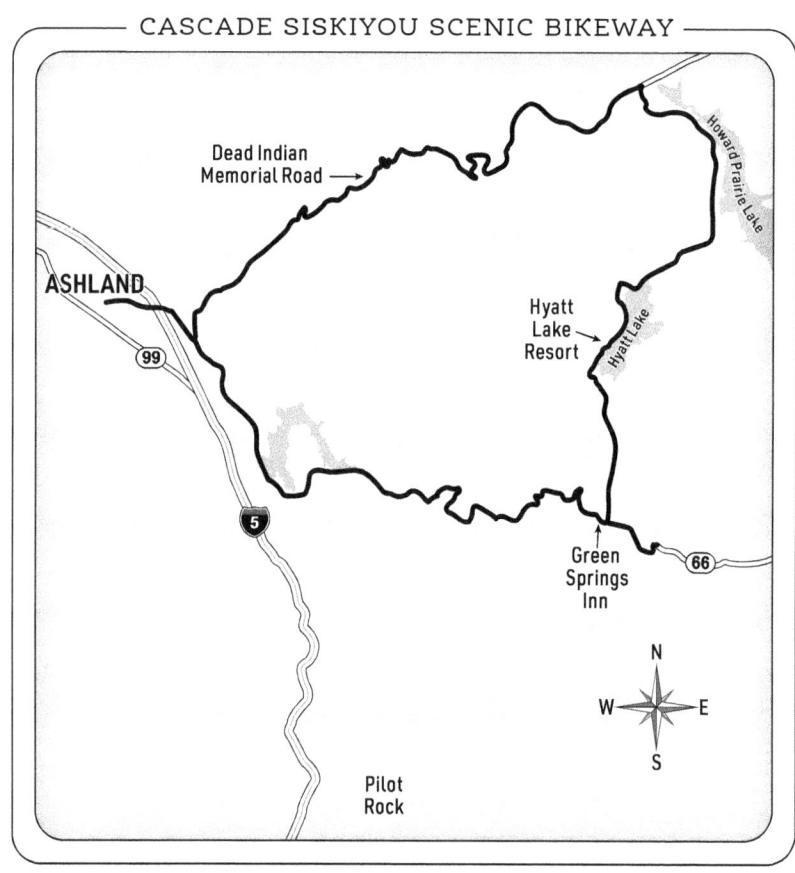

Dead Indian Memorial Road

ASHLAND

99

5

Hyatt Lake Resort

Hyatt Lake

Howard Prairie Lake

Green Springs Inn

66

Pilot Rock

N
W   E
S

by my fear of falling. I'm no professional cyclist. This is a hobby, a passion, but it's not . . . look out for those rocks . . . worth a trip to an emergency room. I repeatedly squeeze the hand brakes to shave off some speed. My sense of control returns. I continue to rush toward Ashland, and 30 mph is fast enough under these conditions.

Now locked into mental cruise control, it's easy for me to think back about the miles we've already ridden along the 54-mile Cascade Siskiyou Scenic Bikeway.

I always like to visit Ashland. People familiar with the city 15 miles north of the California border likely associate it with the Oregon Shakespeare Festival, the honored repertory theater that stages the works of The Bard and many other playwrights during its multi-production, nine-month season each year. The Oregon Shakespeare Festival with its 1,190-seat Elizabethan Theatre was founded in 1935 and has been the focal point of a vibrant downtown for decades. Add a food and wine scene and Southern Oregon's almost limitless outdoor recreational choices and this becomes one of the state's popular destinations.

The Willamette Valley wine region receives praise for its pinot noir production, but Southern Oregon wine producers can argue their vintages are worthy of equal recognition. The Rogue Valley, Applegate Valley, and Umpqua Valley American Viticultural Areas (AVAs) from Ashland to Roseburg include some of the state's warmest growing conditions as well as cool microclimates. The result is a collection of quality grape varietals, both red and white. Early settler Peter Britt, a famed photographer and horticulturist, planted vines in 1852 in nearby Jacksonville. More than 170 years later, Southern Oregon wines are attracting international attention.

When in Ashland, I like to hike in Lithia Park. I head toward the Shakespeare Festival campus and the city's Downtown Plaza, a small triangle with an information kiosk and public water fountains surrounded by parking spaces. Clustered on any given day are artists, groups of young people who may or may not be passing through town, and street musicians. My trained ear frequently identifies strains of The Grateful Dead.

Once into the park, which abuts the plaza, numerous paths follow Ashland Creek past a playground, rose garden, tennis courts, a duck pond, and other amenities on the way to a swimming reservoir. It's also easy to slip away from the structured park and follow dirt trails into the hills.

Ashland also is home to Southern Oregon University, located a mile and a half down Siskiyou Boulevard, the city's primary north-south street. The city has prioritized bicycling as a mode of transportation, making it safe and convenient for cyclists to get around.

We took a detour yesterday on our way to Ashland to ride around the big caldera inside Crater Lake National Park. Rim Drive around Crater Lake is not a scenic bikeway, though one may argue it's the most beautiful ride in the state. Here are 33 miles of grueling climbs and sweeping downhills, 33 miles with very little flat road to be found. The road either goes up or down.

A route from Klamath Falls up and around Crater Lake did not make the cut when proposed to scenic bikeway evaluators. There were sound reasons for rejection, proponents and committee members have told me, including the reality that some portion of Rim Drive needs repairs almost every year. That was clear to us as we descended in the rain along the south side of the lake. Road conditions were horrendous.

That doesn't stop thousands of cyclists who show up on two Saturdays each September for Ride the Rim events when a significant portion of the two-lane road is closed to all motorized vehicles. The event, at dizzying elevations reaching 8,000 feet, is staged so riders can experience the park without the noise and exhaust of internal combustion engines.

"The natural quiet of the park is one of its most outstanding features," says Crater Lake National Park Superintendent Craig Ackerman. "Cyclists, hikers, skaters, and runners can all appreciate the park in a more natural setting and be safer while they negotiate the twists and turns. Virtually everyone who has participated said it was the experience of a lifetime, not duplicated elsewhere."

For the record, Crater Lake is not a lake. The caldera we call Crater Lake was created more than 7,700 years ago when Mount Mazama erupted in what volcanologists conclude was one of the largest geologic events in the past 12,000 years. The volcano exploded for three days and once the core of the mountain was expelled, the remaining top collapsed leaving a catch basin with no natural streams in or out, a bowl that collects rain and snowmelt with no pollutants, no sediment, no mineral deposits flowing in.

The lake, the deepest in the United States at 1,943 feet, appears vibrantly blue. All other color wavelengths are absorbed in the water, and only blue is visible to the eye.

We completed our lap around the lake, stopping as often as possible to enjoy the views and rest our legs. Circling Crater Lake is part physical, part mental, and part pilgrimage. It's more than a bike ride.

Our ride today starts at Ashland Hills Hotel & Suites on the far eastern edge of the city where we stayed overnight. Misha and Robert left the day before so now four of us, Bob, Patti, Eric, and I, prepare to start. This bikeway officially begins and ends at Garfield Park, a small neighborhood green spot two miles to the west. Bob and Eric quickly pull away and move out of sight while Patti and I brace for what's ahead.

The Strava app rates our climb up the Green Springs Highway a Category 1 hill. We have seven miles of twists and turns with a 6 percent average road gradient. Nice and easy, I remind myself. Keep the chain spinning nice and easy.

Green Springs Highway, or Highway 66, curves its way up the side of a hill with one tight turn after another. The surface pitches at steep angles with each bend to the right, and, as hard as we're working now, pedaling out those steep corners seems insurmountable. Fortunately, the road is so narrow and the turns so snug that cars and trucks can't gain speed. And like our ride up to McKenzie Pass in June, we can hear the sounds of engines roar up the canyon long before vehicles reach us. We take advantage and slide near the center line to avoid the deep dips.

There's a tree ahead offering some shade, so Patti and I stop. To the south in the distance is Cascade-Siskiyou National Monument land. We can see the top of far-off Pilot Rock, a volcanic plug near the California border. Magma slowed and eventually blocked what geologists call the throat of a volcano about 25 million years ago. Erosion over time exposed this hardened lava, this plug called Pilot Rock. Travelers in the mid-1800s used the landmark to guide or pilot their way to and from California. If there were a bench here, I might have stopped longer to simply sit and stare across the ridgelines. Our only seats today, however, are 6x8-inch wood guardrail posts that suffice for a break, but not much more.

We start again, riding a couple miles and taking a break, repeating this process until we finally crest the Green Springs Mountain summit, elevation 4,551 feet, the road sign says. We're once again intersecting the Pacific Crest Trail. After an obligatory summit sign selfie, Patti and I push on to the Green Springs Inn two miles ahead where we know Eric and Bob are relaxing. We eventually cross a gravel parking lot and see them sitting on large boulders placed in front of the inn.

The Green Springs Inn is a two-story building with a log cabin vibe. A long porch reaches across the front with wood siding stained dark brown. There's an open patio on the north side with room for seven or eight tables. Umbrellas provide shade when the nearby evergreens don't. I remember a previous visit here when we sat on the patio among bike, motorcycle, and car travelers as we guzzled pitchers of ice water faster than our server could bring them out. We ordered pie as is our habit, though I now can't remember what I requested. It likely was hot apple with a small scoop of vanilla ice cream, my go-to pie order. Did Bob get the rhubarb?

We arrive today before the restaurant opens, so we won't be having pie this time. No pitchers of ice water, either. The inn, however, installed a water dispenser embedded in an exterior wall by the front door. We fill, drink, and refill.

There's another water source a mile and a half down the hill if we're willing to work for it. An underground spring, now called Tub Springs State Wayside, likely dates back centuries and probably served native peoples long before immigrants stopped here to water their oxen. The name Tub Springs was attached in the 1930s after stone tubs were built. Those tubs have been upgraded over the decades and three stone cisterns remain there today. Pipes also were installed to make the water easily accessible.

The water is safe to drink, a Jackson County Parks official tells me later because a UV light is used to disinfect the water, cleansing it of microbiological contamination, as per Oregon Health Authority requirements. The water is also tested quarterly.

Our next stop, Hyatt Reservoir, is nearly five miles away. After a long climb up to the Green Springs Inn, one would hope the hard work is behind us. Not so; there's more elevation gain before we arrive at the reservoir. We follow the narrow and lightly used East Hyatt Lake Road through groves of juniper trees until we reach a junction welcoming us to the federal Bureau of Land Management's Hyatt Lake Recreation Area. Our designated route angles left on Hyatt Dam Road.

There's a hiking path emerging from the trees both left and right of us. It's the Pacific Crest Trail again. We catch glimpses of water ahead as we casually ride toward the reservoir's west edge. With final left-then-right bends in the road, cabins with green metal roofs appear. A banner strung between two towering junipers exclaims "Bikers Welcome."

"They must mean us," Eric jokes, pointing out evidence to the contrary. Motorcycles are parked at the Hyatt Lake Resort.

The resort is a collection of 25 privately owned cabins available to renting visitors. The units are more like comfortable condos than rustic cabins. Some have views of the reservoir, a water source for

Ashland and Jackson County. Others look west into the national forest. The reservoir's water level is low, in part because recent dam upgrades required officials to release more water than normal. Ongoing drought conditions in Southern Oregon have also taken a toll. In good years, the reservoir is a fishing destination with its rainbow trout, largemouth bass, and crappie populations. In bad years such as this, the resort's guests are mushroom hunters in the spring, elderberry pickers in the late summer, bikers of all kinds, and families simply looking to get away.

We find Pearl, a 30s-something mother of two, behind the resort store's cash register. She happily greets us, answering questions and knowingly pointing to snacks she knows cyclists seek: salty chips, M&Ms, Coca-Cola, Gatorade. She's seen it all before.

We pay and find a table on the patio. A young woman 10 feet away is carefully sorting socks, protein bars, toothpaste, and more between a cardboard box and a backpack heavily ladened with everything one might need to survive in the wilderness. I've read the book *Wild* by Oregonian Cheryl Strayed and I've seen the movie. It's obvious to us this woman, like Cheryl, is on a personal mission.

"Are you hiking the Pacific Crest Trail?" I ask, curious to know all about her adventure yet wary of prying.

"Yes," she says with a slight smile.

"Where are you from?"

"Los Angeles."

"How's it going so far?"

"Good," she says, her fingers flipping the pages of a well-worn paperback book. Her destination is Cascade Locks on the Columbia River and the Bridge of the Gods, a steel bridge connecting Oregon and Washington State.

Hikers are commonplace at the Hyatt Lake Resort, Pearl says. "We are an official restocking site for the Pacific Crest Trail. The trail comes within a half mile of us. We may be one of the closest places to the trailhead for package drops."

Pearl has seen many hikers during her three years at the resort, but one explorer is memorable. "I had a lady who said she started the trail in 1968 and she was only able to hike 200 miles before she broke her leg," Pearl recalls. "She came back last summer to complete it. She was 91 years old and this was something she dreamed of finishing. She said this was the only thing left on her bucket list."

As Pearl tells it, the woman first started her quest from the California-Mexico border and barely made it into the mountains east of Riverside, Calif., when that broken leg ended her effort. More than 50 years later, she returned to finish her journey. "She said she had trained for three years to get her stamina and ability up."

Was she doing this alone?

No, Pearl says, the woman arranged to have friends accompany her on designated trail segments. As one person completed a section, another would be there to take over. "And, she broke her wrist in the Sierras," Pearl says. The petite woman, a little more than 5 feet tall and 110 pounds, is carrying a pack on her back and she now has a broken wrist. She was going to complete the trail. It was only a broken wrist this time.

"She really made an impact on me," Pearl says. "If you really want to do something, you can do it. She was such an inspiration."

We leave the resort rested and ready for our final 26 miles, starting with a pass by Howard Prairie Lake, another water reservoir. We emerge from the trees to see Mount McLoughlin in the distance. It's been an estimated 20,000 years since this volcano blew. Immigrant settlers named the landmark after John McLoughlin, the 1820s superintendent or head of Hudson Bay Company trading operations in what was then called Oregon Country. State history best remembers McLoughlin as an advocate for American interests in the region and a business owner in Oregon City at the end of the Oregon Trail. He's called the "Father of Oregon." His statue is in the Capitol Visitor Center in Washington, D.C. It's one of two statues honoring Oregonians in the U.S. Capitol. The other is missionary and pioneer Jason Lee. Coincidentally, both Lee and McLoughlin were born in what is now the province of Quebec, Canada.

We eventually turn west onto Dead Indian Memorial Road for a final climb and our high-speed downhill run to Ashland. The name Dead Indian Memorial Road has been the subject of local government debate for many years. The road is an alternative route from Ashland to Lake of the Woods, Upper Klamath Lake, and Crater Lake National Park. Attempts have been made over the years to change the road's name in deference to descendants of native peoples living in the area. Local accounts suggest the term used for the road and other nearby locations derived from an incident when early white settlers in the area discovered the bodies of two people near a local creek. In 1993, according to local media reports, the word "memorial" was added to the road name. Later efforts to change the road's name have been unsuccessful.

The road rises before us. Eric and Bob again break away while Patti and I do our slow thing until we eventually reach the top. Everyone pulls food from jersey pockets. I finish a thick slice of Carla's homemade banana bread, sustenance for the final miles.

We then descend those final 13 miles, some of it across the loose aggregate rocks of that unfinished chip seal project. The road twists and turns as we drop nearly 3,400 feet.

We're back in Ashland.

(13)

'Turn Around and Look Behind You'
Twin Bridges Scenic Bikeway

• • •

Start and Finish: Downtown Bend
Distance: 36 miles
Elevation Gain: 1,812 feet
Rating: Moderate

Bend – August 19, 2021

The Deschutes River is Central Oregon's crown jewel. From its origin at Little Lava Lake in the mountains southwest of Bend, waters flow south to Wickiup Reservoir, collect there and then reverse course north through the city and onto the Columbia River. The Deschutes is a haven for wildlife, it's a source for hydroelectric power, and it's the region's outdoor playground. Fishing, boating, rafting, and kayaking are huge water-based activities here.

As I lift my bike from its car rack, I see tranquil water in Bend's downtown Drake Park. Mirror Pond was created when the Bend Water, Light and Power Company constructed the Newport Avenue dam between 1910 and 1913 to generate hydro-electricity. The dam still regulates river water flow and powers the community more than a century later. This is the Deschutes River at perhaps its most peaceful point.

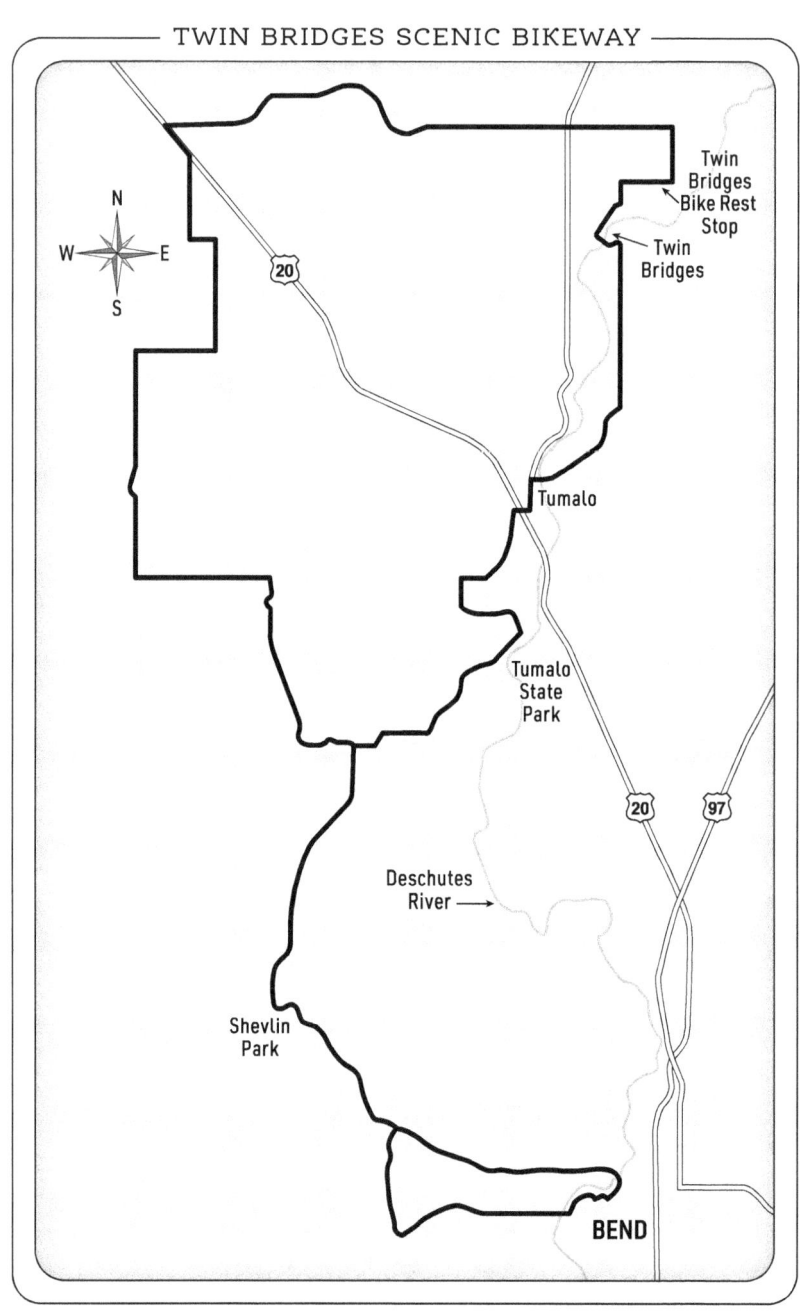

TWIN BRIDGES SCENIC BIKEWAY

N
W · E
S

20

Twin
Bridges
Bike Rest
Stop

Twin
Bridges

Tumalo

Tumalo
State
Park

20   97

Deschutes
River →

Shevlin
Park

BEND

Carla and I are visiting family in Bend for a few days, and I have an opportunity to complete two more scenic bikeways while we're here. The first is the Twin Bridges Scenic Bikeway, a comfortable ride from downtown Bend. The city's bike lane network makes it easy to navigate through town and I quickly find myself passing Shevlin Park and gliding down Johnson Road northwest of town.

Shevlin Park, like Mirror Pond, is woven into the community fabric. The 900-acre park, featuring Tumalo Creek and old-growth forest, has been a year-round recreation destination since the Shevlin-Hixon Lumber Company donated the first parcel of land to the city in 1919. (Tom Shevlin, company founder, was a Yale football star from 1902 through 1905, a four-time All-American, a national celebrity, and an early member of the College Football Hall of Fame.)

Johnson Road turns to Tyler Road where horse ranches and long blankets of bucolic green grass contrast the rough stumble of nearby sagebrush. I maneuver my way north with a sequence of 90-degree turns until I reach the McKenzie-Bend Highway nearly 16 miles from the start.

Cycling is a solitary activity. You can ride with a group or head out by yourself, but you always will find yourself alone with the rhythms of self-propelling motion. I recall how Bob and I followed these roads in 2018, how the west wind chilled us on that April day. While I like the camaraderie of riding with friends, I also welcome these moments.

In time, local cyclists appear in ones and twos. Some overtake me, some get overtaken, and others pedal by in the opposite direction. Yet here I am again. Alone. Happily so.

Stopping at an intersection, two riders by the side of the road interject the first voices I've heard for miles. They explain that these roads are popular with local cyclists. "Turn around and look behind you," one says. To the west, the peaks of the Cascade Range appear in a line for review. Lingering snow at the highest elevations of the Three Sisters and Broken Top shines in the midday summer sun. I gaze, stare a little longer, and then turn back to smile my thanks.

Look away from the mountains and the scenery becomes a constant. Ponderosa pines and open fields interrupt the sage. Small hills and distant buttes punctuate the horizon. I now ride these flat roads uninterrupted, eventually moving along Innes Market Road and White Rock Loop Road before a graceful bend sweeps west. I pedal for another minute, a little more than the length of a football field, and come across a bright purple picnic table centered under a large sun umbrella. It's a roadside rest for cyclists.

"This was always a frequently used route," Bob Haas says, explaining the genesis of his Twin Bridges Bike Aid Station. "People were stopping here on their own just to rest and look at the mountain views."

When the state included the road past his house as part of this bikeway in 2012, the lifelong bike rider decided he needed to act. "I wondered what could potentially help bikers to make it more enjoyable."

People were already stopping here, he thought. Why not create a way station to make these pauses a little more comfortable? Bob decided to create a place to sit, rest, and enjoy the views. Deschutes County granted permission for a right-of-way between Bob's property and the road. A neighbor donated a tire pump and bike repair station now anchored in concrete with screwdrivers, wrenches, and other handy emergency tools tethered to a metal stand. "She was looking for a location to install it and I convinced her this would be a good spot."

A picnic table was donated by Tumalo Coffeehouse. Webcyclery in Bend provided some spare tire tubes. Visit Bend, a local tourism marketing group, added small bottles of sunscreen and a first aid kit.

"It organically grew," he says. "Everything happened within the first year."

That was 2014.

This is my stop today. Thankfully, I don't need the repair tools. I open a mailbox attached to the picnic table to see sunscreen, the first aid kit, and tubes. Two older bikes are permanently racked atop a wood-and-wire fence. A wooden sign nailed to the fence displays a stylish font in purple reading "Twin Bridges Bike Aid Station." Nancy Haas, Bob's wife, made the sign using a neighbor's reclaimed barn wood.

"It's really been a fun project," Bob says. "Initially, we had a lot of Central Oregon riders stop by, probably because of the novelty of it. Folks from out of town frequently stop here still. They're really intrigued by it. I'll sometimes go out and talk with them. When different people stop and don't know each other, it's easy to get into conversation."

Some riders over the years have paid forward Bob's generosity by leaving energy bars for others who may need something to eat. Others have made small monetary donations, perhaps as payment for a new tube or a Band-Aid. "And, a few people wrote notes that were really nice."

I relax at the purple picnic table, staring down a narrow two-lane road pointing due west to the Cascades. Here are three minutes of silence.

I ask Bob Haas if he's aware that public interest in his aid station has reached the point that its location is pinned on Google Maps. Unaware until now, he accepts the designation. "It's a part of the local cycling community," he simply responds. "It serves a role."

I pedal on over the namesake twin bridges spanning the Deschutes River at mile 22.5 and south toward the town of Tumalo, an unincorporated corner of Deschutes County only seven miles north of downtown Bend. I have my mind set on a short latte and a cinnamon raisin bagel so I glide to a stop in front of the Tumalo Coffeehouse, collect my order, and settle down at a shaded patio table. Pickup trucks and SUVs consistently rumble by, and I surmise this is the daily traffic flow.

Tumalo took form in the early 20th century on the backs of would-be farmers who staked claims on this arid land, according to the Oregon Historical Society's Oregon History Project. Crops required plenty of water, of course, but the water table was hundreds of feet below in many places making drilling difficult. Attempts at managing irrigation districts failed as well and farming never took root. But downtown Tumalo bustles today as part of the greater Bend area.

Rested, I brace for the final nine miles, remounting my bike, carefully crossing Highway 20, and passing near Tumalo State Park as I head toward Mirror Pond.

⑭

'It Never Gets Old'

Sisters to Smith Rock Scenic Bikeway

• • •

Start and Finish: Sisters or Smith Rock State Park
Distance: 36 miles
Elevation Gain: 960 feet from Sisters,
1,315 from Smith Rock
Rating: Moderate

Sisters – August 20, 2021

Sisters' Village Green Park is quiet. The place was crowded with cyclists excited to climb into the Cascades when we were here two months ago, but today the grassy square is empty except for small children scurrying about a playground under their parents' watchful eyes. This is the starting point for both the McKenzie Pass and Sisters to Smith Rock scenic bikeways, and I'm here to ride east to one of Oregon's most popular state parks.

At 36 miles, this can be one of the region's most relaxing rides. With a few short climbs as outliers, this is a comfortable high desert outing with the requisite sagebrush and Ponderosa pines. The rewards at the end of my day are a bench, a long drink, and an astonishing view of the cliffs inside Smith Rock State Park.

Or should I have gone the other way? Should I have started at Smith Rock and ridden to Sisters? Logistics dictate a ride back

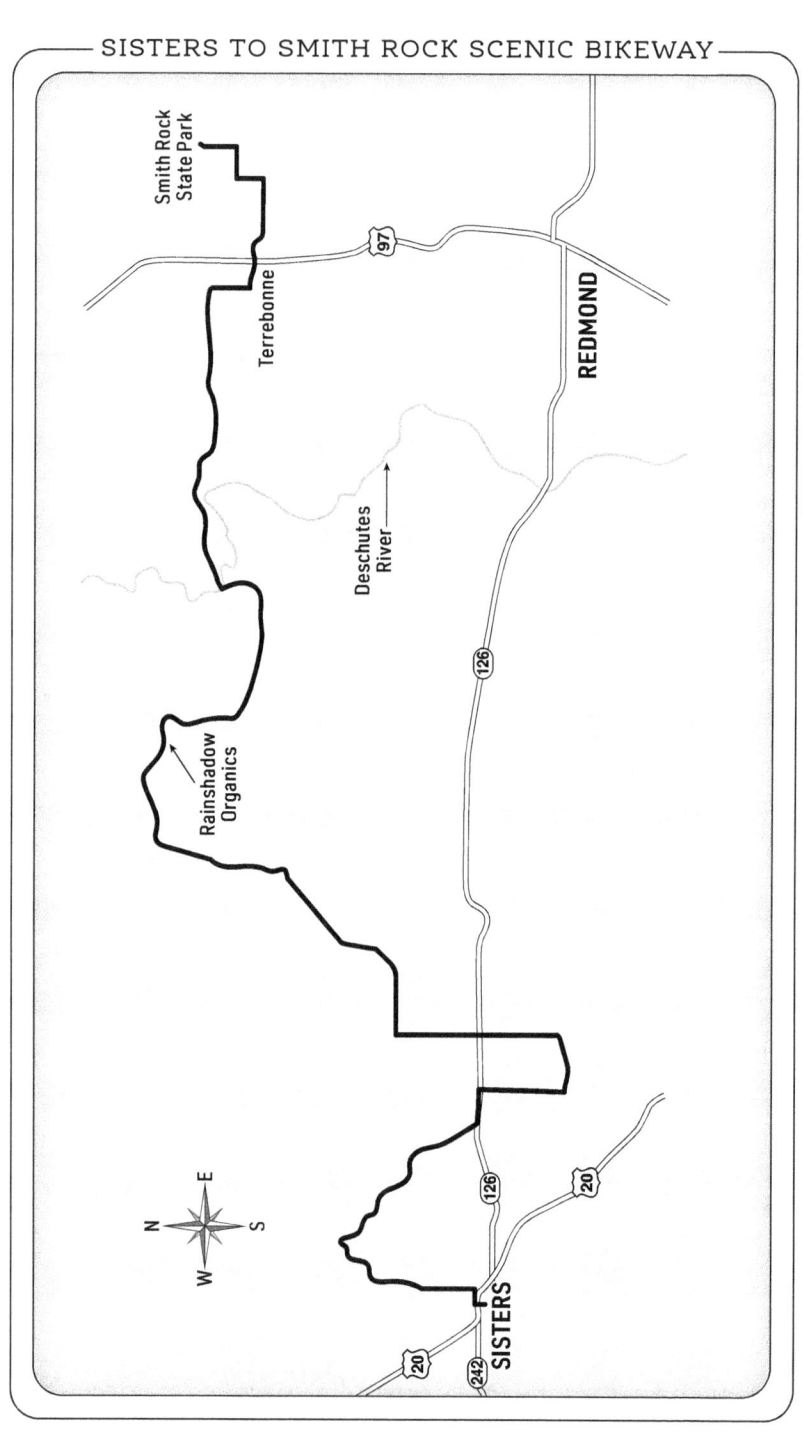

to the start is required in either scenario unless you are prepared to transform an otherwise pleasant day on the bike into a long, tiring, 72-mile round trip.

Brad Boyd, owner of Eurosports in Sisters, may suggest that finishing the day in his hometown is a good idea. For starters, it's easy to clean up and recover here before moving on to other festivities. "You can have a nice shower," he says, noting a coin-operated shower is located in the Village Green public facilities building. "Now you feel refreshed and maybe you'll want to stay in Sisters a little longer."

Brad advocates making Sisters a cycling vacation destination. Drive here, park your car, and stay awhile, he says. Four days sounds good to him.

"If you're a cyclist, you could do a different ride every day. You could walk to Sisters Coffee Company, have a cup of coffee, and then get out and go for your ride," he says. "You can walk to dinner afterward, do some shopping, and you would not need to get in your car. Is Sisters gonna have great nightlife? No, but I'd find it pretty relaxing and chill. I don't need nightlife after a day's ride."

Carla is headed to Smith Rock State Park by car so I'm riding from Sisters.

The road north from Sisters quickly transitions from small town to ranchettes, from farmland to stands of trees, from a golf course to high plains until Holmes Road leads to Rainshadow Organics, a farm and store midway between Sisters and Terrebonne. The farm is owned and operated by Sarahlee Lawrence, who grew up here but left in 1999 to see the world. She became a professional river guide and successfully navigated rapids around the globe before she felt the pull to return home. She's been running the 100-acre farm and adjacent 650-acre cattle ranch since 2010 and chronicles her story in her memoir *River House*.

"I found my way back," Sarahlee tells me. "I came home to raise food."

Rainshadow Organics provides what Sarahlee calls a "full diet" Community Support Agriculture (CSA) program for 300 subscribing Central Oregon families. Full diet means consumers will receive the nutrition needed for a well-rounded and sustainable diet, she says. And, in a larger sense, the farm is part of her role as a steward of the land.

I steer my bike onto the farm's packed gravel driveway and pedal toward the main building, the farm store where an attractive variety of fresh vegetables and other organic food products are for sale. I buy something to drink as an employee invites me to relax in the shade of the building's large front deck. I accept the offer.

The bikeway crosses the Deschutes River nearly five miles later and eventually reaches the outskirts of unincorporated Terrebonne along Highway 97. There's still one hill to climb, a short but sharp quarter-mile ramp up C Avenue. Once crested, there's a cautious highway crossing and a final push toward Smith Rock.

Hills appear in the distance, jutting from the flat plains as the final three miles pass. Visual details come into focus as I approach along NE 17th Street. Dark and indistinct geography transitions to bright and brown. Clear vertical lines seem chiseled into towering rock walls. Then, finally, a full panoramic introduction to Smith Rock is unveiled over the final 450 yards.

Smith Rock State Park is for hikers, bikers, and climbers. There are miles of trails for mountain bikes and anyone on foot. The most popular walking trail leads from a small parking lot down and into a canyon. Follow the path along a very quiet and narrow Crooked River. Don't be surprised if a bald or golden eagle soars above.

"When you arrive at Smith Rock and you get up close and descend into the canyon, you have a moment of wonder looking up at a 600-foot [rock] spectacle," says park manager Matt Davey. "It makes you feel so small. It shocks you out of your day-to-day mindset. It's almost akin to visiting a national park where you walk up to the rim of a canyon or a beautiful lake and you have a sense that this is breathtaking and way bigger than one person."

The park is perhaps best known for rock climbers who travel from all over the world to test themselves on these walls. Matt estimates nearly 200,000 climbers make their way to Smith Rock each year to scale more than 2,000 routes using ropes and bolts embedded in the stone.

"Smith Rock was put on the map when sport climbing developed here," he says.

Here's what we know about Smith Rock. Volcanic ash and debris expelled from volcanic eruptions accumulated here over millions of years, compacting, and hardening over time into what is called volcanic tuff. The Crooked River then did its part, flowing through and gradually eroding softer layers and leaving the harder cliffs and pinnacles standing.

Here's what we don't know. Historians often say the formation is named after John Smith, a Linn County sheriff who was credited in 1867 by a Willamette Valley newspaper with "discovering" it. The Oregon State Parks website, however, also gives credence to a theory that it's named after Pvt. Volk Smith, a soldier who fell to his death here during a battle in 1863.

Here's what Matt Davey knows. "I look forward every day to looking at these rocks and seeing how the lights change on them. It never gets old."

The day's ride complete, I find a seat overlooking the canyon, the footpath, and those towering rock formations. With some food, water, and this stunning view, I consider this a ride well spent.

Vernonia's Rail Trail
Tualatin Valley Scenic Bikeway

• • •

Start and Finish: Hillsboro or Vernonia
Distance: 51 miles
Elevation Gain: 1,647 feet from Hillsboro,
1,191 feet from Vernonia
Rating: Moderate

Hillsboro – September 24, 2021

Many of Oregon's scenic bikeways begin in remote parts of the state. Lakeview is remote. Port Orford is remote. Hillsboro is not.

Hillsboro, on the western edge of metropolitan Portland, is home to what some call the Silicon Forest. International computer chipmaker Intel is here. So is Adobe, McAfee, Salesforce, and Oracle. Then there's Nike, with its worldwide headquarters next door in Beaverton. More than 1,800 Nike employees work in Hillsboro as well.

Start pedaling from Rood Bridge Park on the city's south side, however, and the transition from suburban to rural is immediate. There are no sprawling office campuses out here. No residential neighborhoods. Open fields, farms, nurseries, and eventually vineyards await.

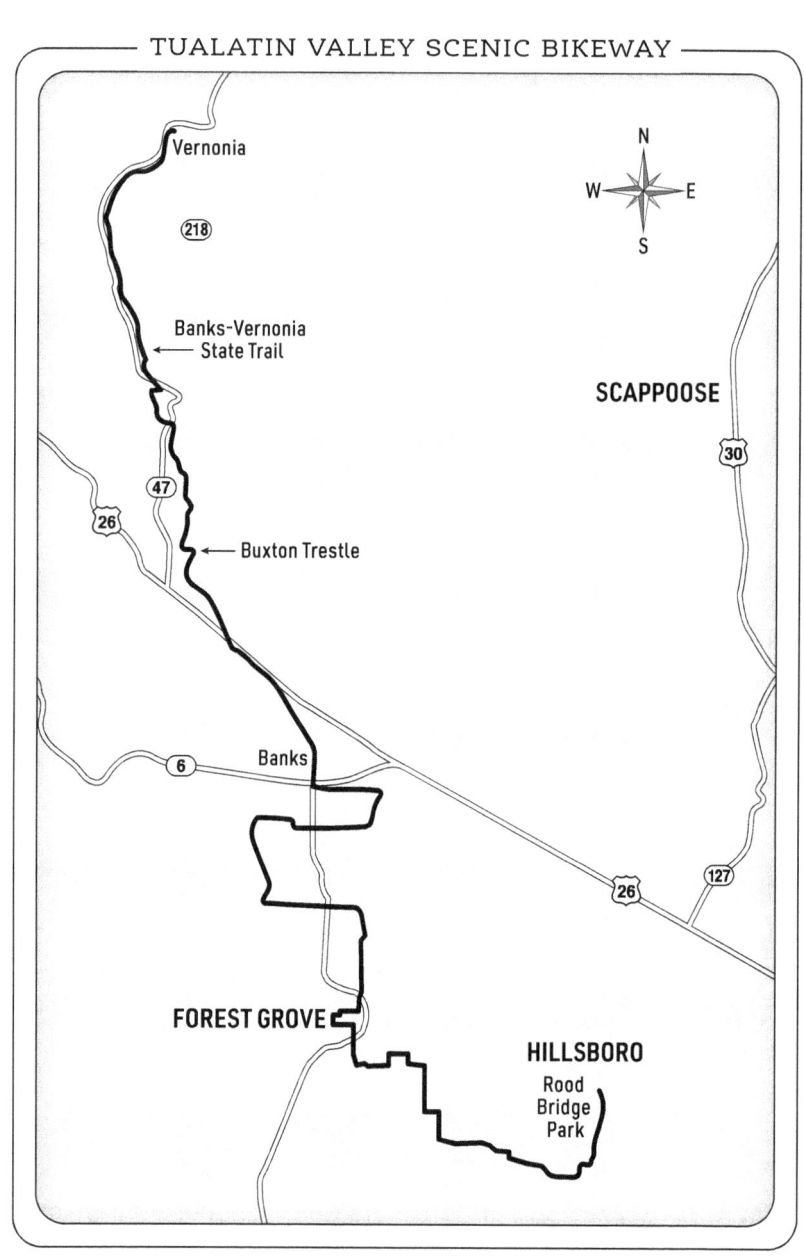

TUALATIN VALLEY SCENIC BIKEWAY

Vernonia

218

Banks-Vernonia
State Trail

SCAPPOOSE

30

47

26

Buxton Trestle

6   Banks

26   127

FOREST GROVE

HILLSBORO
Rood
Bridge
Park

N
W   E
S

The Tualatin Valley is one of those lesser-known regions in Oregon. I doubt many international tourists have the Tualatin Valley on their destination bucket lists. Yet this area is much like other parts of Oregon in that quality wines and good beers are produced here, and local tourism marketers work hard to raise the regional profile and spread the word.

It's a worthwhile cause. There's much to do in the Tualatin Valley and Washington County. There are glider flights, helicopter rides, a zipline, and Pumpkin Ridge Golf Club, a course made famous in 1996 when Tiger Woods won his third consecutive amateur golf championship here. Still, the valley is likely best known for its craft breweries and wineries.

Patti and I are again joined by Rose Owens, who did a turn on the Willamette Valley bikeway earlier in the year. Today's ride starts flat and easy from Hillsboro to Forest Grove past the farms, hazelnut orchards, Christmas tree farms, and the ever-present wild blackberry bushes. We arrive in Forest Grove less than 13 miles later.

The land now known as Forest Grove originally was home to the Kalapuya tribe until European immigrants arrived and claimed it as their own. First, there were Alvin and Abigail Smith, then the Clarks, and the Littlejohns in the 1840s, according to a posted history by the City of Forest Grove. The rest, as one may say, is history.

The Rev. Harvey Clark arrived in 1844 and, with Alvin Smith, started a Congregational church. Clark and teacher Tabitha Brown created the Tualatin School in 1849 for local children as a way to attract more settlers. They eventually added a college and Pacific University began offering classes in 1854. Nearly 170 years later, that private university enrolls about 3,850 students across four Willamette Valley campuses.

We roll through Forest Grove and head back into open countryside, zigzagging along quiet, rural roads until we arrive in the farm community of Banks. It's less than a mile between a streetlight on the south end of Main Street and the Banks-Vernonia State Trail.

We've ridden 30 miles and we've seen enough farmland for one day, so we're excited for a change. The Banks-Vernonia State Trail, a 20-mile rail-to-trail path managed by Oregon State Parks, is the first of its kind in Oregon. Trains once carried timber from Vernonia and Columbia County along this way. Railroad tracks have been replaced by an 8-foot-wide asphalt path for hikers, joggers, and bicyclists to travel between Banks and the town of Vernonia without interference from anything motorized.

The trail is never steep, but a near-constant slight tilt uphill. There are benches along the way where people can sit, rest, and enjoy time in the woods. At one point, we pass two bike riders who parked at the edge of a small, square piece of grass and laid down on their backs looking skyward. We roll by but they don't seem to notice, perhaps transfixed on clouds. It would be nice, I think as we go by, to stop and do nothing for a few minutes. No moving, no talking, just staring up and listening to the wind rustling the trees.

We shun impromptu rest stops, making our way toward the Buxton Trestle, a crossing originally built in 1920 for trains to pass over Mendenhall Creek. The trestle, now part of the state trail, spans a 773-foot gap 80 feet above the ground. I can't recall seeing anything like it in more than 10 years of cycling so I take pictures as we cross. No, it has to be video. I activate the phone camera and go first, pointing the phone backwards to capture images of Patti riding behind me. At the far end, I review the video and realize my camera angle isn't right. We have to do this again, I say, trying to make my statement sound more like a request than an expectation. Patti knows; she's been a featured cyclist in my photos and videos all summer. We go back and start again, this time with Patti leading the way. The video works and it's on social media by the end of the day.

The crossing itself is smooth and safe. A solid, 8-foot-wide bridge deck provides plenty of space for bicyclists or hikers to pass. Wooden sidings perhaps five feet high stand guard for anyone with a fear of heights.

The trail eventually crests just north of L.L. Stub Stewart State Park and we begin our gradual descent into Vernonia. I decided miles ago that I love this trail and I'm already making mental notes to bring Carla and Sam here. Rose drove ahead and is waiting in Anderson Park, the car positioned under shady evergreens. Bikes racked and equipment stored, we make our way a few blocks to Bridge Street, Vernonia's main street, and find a picnic table for lunch at The Black Bear Coffee Company and the adjacent Black Iron Grill. Sandwiches quickly arrive and our server sets down our food before hurrying to greet arriving friends. Her enthusiasm leads me to wonder if these heartfelt hugs are the result of a long, COVID-mandated separation. Or, is it simply the nature of friendship here in this rural forest community?

Whenever I think of Vernonia, I'm reminded of Ben Schorzman, a former co-worker who spent nearly 11 childhood years here. I email Ben after the ride to tell him about my afternoon in his hometown. We swap messages and a Q&A session begins. He endorses our stop at the Black Bear, calling it "one of the best things to happen for our downtown."

"I remember when Black Bear opened," Ben writes. "We finally had a coffee shop, a quick lunch place, and a place to sit and enjoy the free Wi-Fi. They created such a welcoming place downtown for people to drop by on their way through."

Vernonia is a small community about 30 miles from Hillsboro and a world away from urban life. Ben describes the community with terms like simple, blue collar, timber, spacious, and conservative.

"During the logging boom of the early and mid-1900s, the town was full of money," Ben says. "There was a working mill. Many of the families in town were connected to the timber industry in some fashion. Even after the mill closed, logging was still a very common job. If you didn't care to go to college, you'd probably end up working as a choker setter on a local crew. It's just the circle of life in a small town with one main industry."

A definition: A choker setter fastens chains or steel cables, the chokers, around logs that will be dragged from the forest by tractor or another device. It's a dangerous job.

Ben shares a description for forest communities such as Vernonia: Misunderstood.

"I find Vernonians and people in the logging industry get pigeonholed into a place where others view them as against environmental protections. Honestly, that could not be further from the truth," he says. "When you grow up amongst the trees, you learn to appreciate them even more. You understand the cycle of nature and how you can sustainably harvest timber to earn a living while also being a steward of the land. That's the thing people forget."

Loggers have been working this land for generations, he says, planting at least three saplings for every one harvested tree. They constantly consider how their work affects animal habitats and watersheds. "Loggers know more about nature than almost every hiker, backpacker, and so-called naturalist I've ever met."

Ben did not become a choker setter, choosing instead to attend the University of Oregon and become a journalist. We met in 2010 at the *News-Register*, a community newspaper in McMinnville. Ben was a sportswriter, and I was managing the paper's digital media department. Ben moved to the *Register-Guard* in Eugene in 2013 and continued his sports coverage until 2016 when he started working for the City of Eugene's Library, Recreation and Cultural Services department marketing team. Still, he says, Vernonia is in his heart.

"It's hard to convey to other people what it's like being from a place like Vernonia," Ben says. "You move away for college and start mixing with people who grew up in the suburbs and bigger cities who have absolutely no clue that your hometown is even in the state. Over the years, I settled on a speech for these people. 'Yes, it's in Oregon. You know that hump in the northwest corner of the state? Vernonia is almost in the middle of that. We're about 45 minutes outside of Portland on the way to the coast. Yes, my town is smaller than your high school, and, yes, our mascot was the Loggers.'"

If someone has heard of Vernonia, it's possibly because the town flooded twice in recent years. The first flood, in February 1996, was triggered by heavy rain and high waters that saturated Western Oregon. Many Willamette Valley cities and towns flooded to some degree that month, but Vernonia made headlines. Another even larger flood swept through in 2007.

"Living in Vernonia means that you can't escape the talk of floods. It has shaped what our town looks like. It shapes our conversations during the rainy season," Ben says. "After a big snow, people worry about how quickly it will melt because that could swell the creek and Nehalem River. If we are projected to get a ton of rain for quite a while, people start watching the level of Rock Creek, which runs right through town. Literally everyone will talk about it."

Ben and his family moved to Vernonia, where his mother, Bonnie Holce, already was a schoolteacher, a few months after the 1996 flood. He had a firsthand view of community recovery.

"My mother's basement music classroom at Washington Grade School was flooded. Her classroom was inundated to almost the ceiling," he recalls. "I remember going in days after the water receded to start helping her clean things, and it was awful in there. The mud marks were above her cabinets. She lost everything. Music books, instruments, risers that kids sat on, records, etc. She had to start completely over. And, because we live in a country where teachers are forced to pay for supplies and stuff beyond an acceptable margin, my mom also suffered a significant financial loss.

"The '96 flood was super frustrating to me and an early indicator in my life about how certain towns can be left behind if government doesn't help," Ben continues. "Our school district suffered quite a bit from the setback of 1996. Programs that were flourishing all of a sudden had no supplies, and what couldn't be immediately replaced were never given priority again. It took five years for my mother to get new music books for her classroom, meaning kids went through the entirety of grade school without that curriculum. PE equipment wasn't replaced, or it took forever.

Even the cleanliness of the rooms that flooded was never fully satisfactory again. My mother's room languished. Mold issues persisted, and it wasn't until 2004, eight years after the flood, that they finally moved her and other teachers in the basement to a different location because it caused health issues."

The community also changed following the '96 flood. Houses in the floodplain were raised onto higher foundations in preparation for the next big weather event. Emergency equipment was stockpiled.

"The flood became our identity. If people had heard of Vernonia, it was because of the flood," Ben says. "And then came 2007. My family lives up on a hill out of town so my home was safe, but everyone I knew was affected."

Electrical power to the community was out. Waters inside the schools were waist high.

"Friends and their families lost homes. I still get incredibly sad hearing about my brother's best friend's family and how the water rose so rapidly in the middle of the night that they were stuck in the second story of their home and had to punch a hole in the ceiling to get to the attic and then to the roof to escape."

The second flood changed the town forever, Ben says. "The high school was deemed unusable. Same with the middle school and grade school. All were soon demolished. Places where I spent years of my life were erased. For years after, kids spent their time in modular classrooms until the new school was built up on a hill."

Throughout it all, neighbors helped neighbors. That's what friends do.

"Vernonia is still a beautiful place. It doesn't have sweeping views of mountains or the coast but standing up on a hill looking out over hayfields and hillsides of timber is still pretty," Ben says. "The wind passing through the trees and the rush of the river, the solitude and peace are something people who live there cherish. The pace of life isn't something to be demeaned. It's the reason they live there."

(16)

The Geographic Center of the United States

Grande Tour Scenic Bikeway

• • •

Start and Finish: La Grande
Distance: 134 miles
Elevation Gain: 4,546 feet
Rating: Challenging

La Grande – September 30, 2021

It's late September and we still have four scenic bikeways to cover this year. Rose joins Patti and me on a three-bikeway tour across the state. Here's our plan: We start with the Grande Tour bikeway between La Grande and Baker City where we'll need two days to cover 134 miles. We then drive to Pendleton for the night before spending another two days on the Blue Mountain Century bikeway. We finish the trip with a one-day ride on the Sherar's Falls Scenic Bikeway starting and finishing in Maupin.

It's daunting for all of us, and perhaps more so for Rose. Patti and I have ridden a lot of miles since April, but this is Rose's first multi-day road trip with us. I offer encouragement until I remember her quiet confidence. She listens, smiles, and says "we'll see how it goes."

We start in La Grande, working our way south through

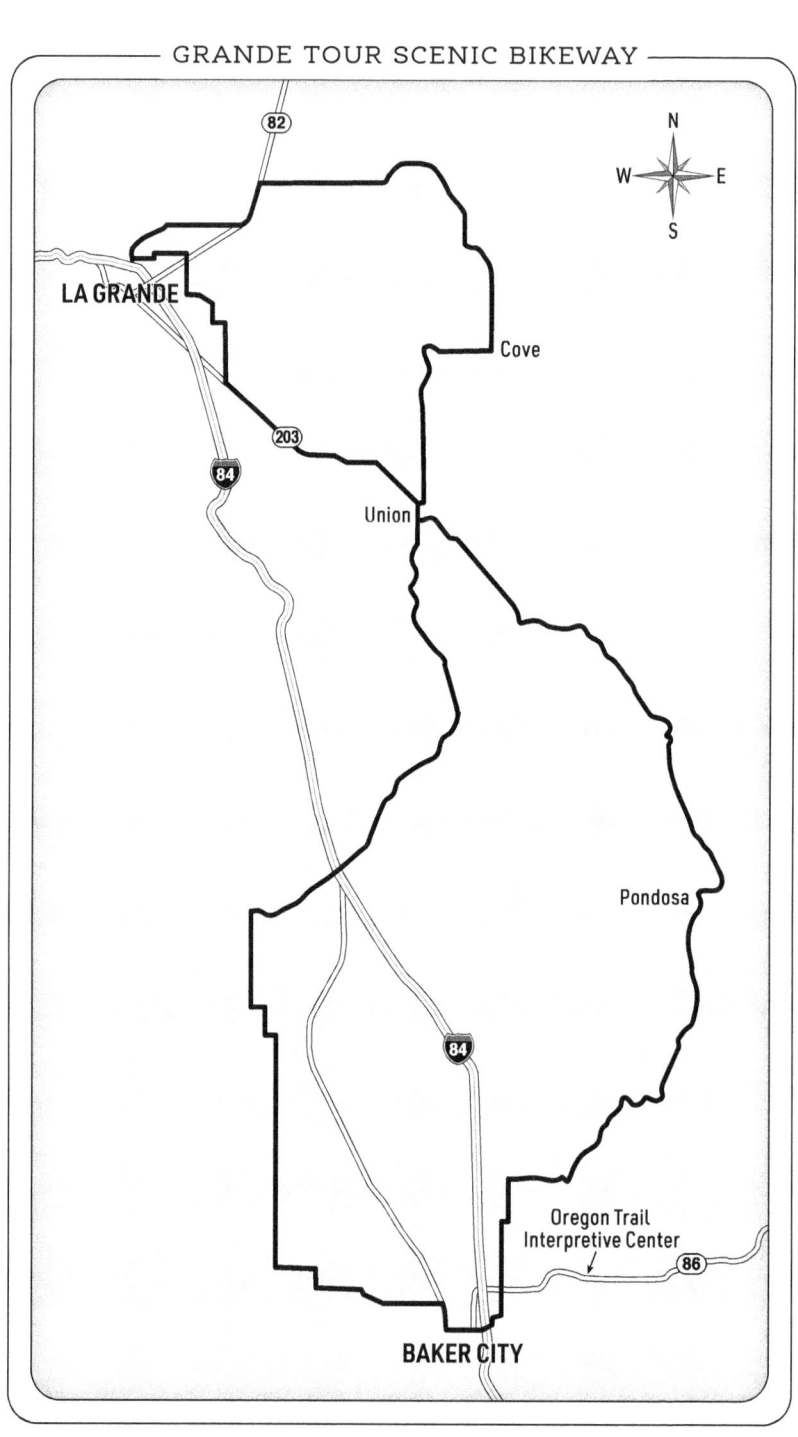

the small town of Union and on to Baker City. That's 60 miles. Rose and I ride first, navigating along city streets before reaching Highway 203 and turning southeast. Our road information forewarned us that traffic on the highway would be heavy. The occasional semi-trailer truck and the frequent pickups do not pose a problem; there is plenty of road shoulder allowing ample room to slide to the right and away from traffic.

But no advance information could predict this forceful headwind. Rose is not deterred, leaning low to catch less air and reduce wind resistance, forcing her small, 44-centimeter bicycle frame into a steady current. We take turns leading, allowing the other to close behind in the slipstream and save energy. I create a much larger slipstream on my 56-centimeter bike and I take longer turns in front. Still, Rose resolutely pedals a fair share of the nine miles.

Researchers disagree on how much energy can be saved while drafting in a slipstream. There are several variables to consider. I've read that a cyclist can save anywhere from 27 to 50 percent effort by drafting. I choose to use an easy-to-remember number—33 percent—and calculate that drafting conserves a third of my energy. With this wind hitting us head on, I'm sliding that percentage even higher.

Throughout it all, Rose perseveres. Better than that, she sets a tone for the next five days. We all will persevere.

We pedal into Union satisfied with our effort and happy to be out of the wind. Patti is waiting for us at the city park and we agree to get sandwiches at the nearby Union Stoplight diner, named in honor of the one illuminated traffic control in town. Adjacent to the park is the historic Union Hotel. We walk over after lunch, climb 10 concrete steps to a veranda, pass through red double doors and step into the lobby. Across the tile floor is a long, high, wooden reception desk. I walk to my left into a parlor and find Charlie Morden, the hotel owner.

Charlie details the Union Hotel's history for me. The building, with its twin wings, was built in 1921 with a red brick exterior. Contrasting off-white brick trims corners and windows. And there are plenty of windows. The original layout included 76 small rooms, each with a double bed, sink, dresser, and a small closet. Shared showers and toilets were down the hall. One hundred years and some remodeling later, there are now 15 rooms, each with its own theme and bathroom.

Charlie's history seems as colorful as many of the rooms. The self-described fifth-generation Oregonian has been an elementary school principal, a home renovation supply store owner, a logger, an outdoor guide, "all those interesting things." And now he's a hotel proprietor. I ask Charlie how he came about owning a hotel.

"The hotel was for sale, and I always wanted one of these," he says, explaining that the building was in foreclosure while he spent six months negotiating with the bank. "We agreed on a price and I bought it. It's been much more than I ever expected it to be, mostly good. The folks who seek out places like this are a very different, fascinating group of folks. They are so enthusiastic that after 100 years it's still here and it hasn't been messed up. The original floors and woodwork are all intact."

The Union Hotel has stood throughout a century of change. "Union is very quiet," he says, reflecting on the place he now calls home. "There were two sawmills in town 100 years ago. The train actually came through Union. There was a flour mill, and I have been told 14 bars and restaurants. It was kind of a self-sustaining place. Now most of the folks who live here work somewhere else. There's no industry in Union anymore. That's all gone now."

Charlie still has Lycra-wearing, bicycle-riding visitors who stop by to see this grand landmark. "We have a couple 'bicycle friendly business' signs in the window," he says. "And, there's room in the basement for bikes. I have had as many as 40 cyclists at a time here. I've had bicyclists in their 90s and bicyclists under 10."

The ride south from Union quickly leads us to more wind. This is not fun, I mutter. Now partnered with Patti, we resume the drafting, alternating "pulls" or turns into the wind. Baker City is still more than three hours away at our pace, and demoralizing thoughts grow even darker when windmills appear on a hill ahead to our left. There's a cluster of these towering machines. I count five windmills, then 10, 20, 22 windmills with long, white, spinning, airplane wing-like blades—visual proof of what we already know. A fierce wind is in our faces.

We have only one option: Ride on.

Even more windmills appear; I have to stop dwelling on the negative. There's supposed to be a downhill grade ahead, so that becomes my motivation, a pin in my mental map. I see the road rise in the distance, an easy climb it seems. If we're lucky, that downhill is just over the crest.

I rewind my conversation with Sam Blake at the Spoke'n Hostel in Mitchell a few months ago. Headwinds were a constant battle as he crossed the continent. "The worst winds I came into were on the Wind River Reservation in Wyoming," he told me. "I hit a wall. I mean, literally, that's how I would describe it. There was no wind, no wind, and then it slammed me and never let up the rest of the day."

Steady breezes with gusts surpassing 30 mph slowed his progress to a mere 5 mph as if he were pedaling up a steep hill. "It was just unbearable," he said. "The last town behind me was 40 miles and the town ahead was 25. What am I going to do?"

He persevered then. We do the same now.

Rose is waiting near the top of the hill. We stop for a moment to rest the legs as she delivers the good news. Indeed, the downhill starts about a quarter mile ahead, she says, and it looks to last a long way. We ride over the top and begin gliding down. The wind no longer concerns us as we quickly roll through the town of North Powder and eventually angle south toward Baker City. To our left is the Elkhorn Wildlife Area, land managed by the Oregon Department of Fish and Wildlife to support Rocky Mountain elk and mule deer seeking food each winter. To our right in the distance is the Blue Mountains' Elkhorn Range where the same deer and elk flourish the rest of the year.

The last 20 miles into Baker City are uneventful, and we ease back into town shortcutting through Geiser Pollman Park and along the city's Leo Adler Memorial Parkway, a hike-and-bike path along the Powder River. The trail was designed as an avenue to view the river, birds, and other wildlife but we're not interested today. Our minds are locked on our motel, the Bridge Street Inn. We're two blocks away and, wait . . . what's that I feel? A flat tire. I walk the bike the rest of the way.

Showered and recovered, and with the tire changed, we take a five-block walk downtown for dinner at Latitude 45 Grille. I marvel each time I visit Baker City. The city's Main Street is extra wide. In fact, a local newspaper publisher here once told me it's wide enough for an extra-long Gold Rush-era mule team to complete a U-turn. While there are no mule teams anymore, they were commonplace in the 1860s when Baker City got its start. Like many Eastern Oregon towns, this place has experienced economic highs and lows. The Victorian architecture popular during the city's heyday remains throughout the downtown historic district.

The 30-room Geiser Grand hotel is the iconic local landmark. Built in 1889, the lavish palace still includes crystal chandeliers, mahogany throughout, and a lobby atrium with a stained-glass roof. It's wonderfully maintained and has earned recognition from the National Trust for Historic Preservation. I stayed here once nearly 20 years ago and now want to show Patti and Rose the ornate interior. Opening the front door, we are immediately met by a hotel employee asking if we are registered guests. We are not, we say, but we just want to look around.

No, she sternly says. Only registered guests are allowed inside. Unfortunate.

Baker City – October 1, 2021

We get an early morning start so we have time to drive seven miles east of downtown Baker City to a small gravel turnout along the north side of Highway 86. We park the car and walk through to a wooden chute leading visitors along a short sidewalk. The asphalt ends and we're suddenly standing on uneven, hard-packed dirt. Small clumps of brush and grass grow on the left and right, but this weathered path is barren. If I close my eyes, I might imagine the sounds of oxen snorting as they pull Prairie

Schooners ladened with possessions and supplies over this soil. Sounds of iron-rimmed wagon wheels might be heard, grinding on axles, and rolling against the ground. Weary travelers could be walking alongside since the vehicle itself has no springs to absorb an extremely bumpy and uncomfortable ride.

These would have been among the sounds heard in this place about 160 years ago. We're standing on the wagon ruts of the Oregon Trail.

Between 300,000 and 500,000 people followed this path from 1841 to 1884 during this nation's largest mass migration, according to the National Historic Oregon Trail Interpretive Center. The ruts created then are still here as evidence, and the federal Bureau of Land Management, keepers of this trail, invite anyone to walk here and step back in time.

I've been here before, but it's a new experience for Rose and Patti. We first drive up a nearby hill to the interpretive center building but it is closed for a major remodel. We're now standing on the path the wagon trains took west from the Snake River, over a ridge and down a wide slope toward Baker City. If you squint, you may think you can see brown lines drawn through the sagebrush. In reality, wagons did not always follow in one line as though it were a lane on an interstate highway. They would travel abreast on open terrain when possible to avoid following in the wake of another wagon's dust.

"It's easy to close your eyes, I think, and imagine yourself there," says Sarah Sherman, the Bureau of Land Management's project manager for the center upgrades. "I think what would be even more powerful is picturing 10 wagons, the sheer amount of people that were coming out between 1860 and 1880. It could have looked like Interstate 84 with traffic. It's hard to imagine the sense of place, how it's changed through time and how that specific place almost feels untouched [today]. That is hard to find these days."

Once it reopens, the interpretive center will again paint a picture, Sarah says. There will be archeological artifacts and museum pieces on display, but the center's ongoing primary goal will be to help people understand what travelers experienced on the Oregon Trail, their struggles, and how they survived after 2,000 miles and five months living off the land.

"People come to us as a landmark not only because we have the physical wagon ruts, but we also like to tell the story. We want to be that cultural and natural history platform, if you will, for people to come and engage with because it is a different story," she says.

"Our exhibits focus on life on the trail and what it meant to take up this journey," Sarah continues. "We also have some discovery areas and interactive components. As you weave your way through the narrative, it takes you on the trail as everyone else did, and you grasp the vision of a day in the life."

We return to Geiser Pollman Park in Baker City to resume our own trail. The road signs lead us east from the city and then north on Atwood Road. Atwood becomes Lindley Road where heavy-duty truck traffic has severely deteriorated the surface quality. It's my turn to drive and I sympathetically watch as Rose and Patti steer their bikes to avoid jarring bumps and potholes. Asphalt disappears altogether; it's now gravel for the next two miles. Finally, with relief, they turn onto the smooth pavement of Highway 203 and continue across the Eastern Oregon plains.

I pull the car to the side of the road and study the route details. Just as we have intersected the Pacific Crest Trail at different points throughout the summer, I think we just crossed the approximate path of the Oregon Trail. While the 20th century Pacific Crest hiking trail is clearly mapped with road signs, the trail that 19th century travelers followed is not distinctly defined today. I think the Oregon Trail may have crossed Lindley Road.

By 10 a.m., 15 miles into our day, I find a gravel turnout just as the highway crests a hill. There's plenty of space to pull the car to the side and wait for the others. As I step out and catch a cool, brisk breeze, I can't remember seeing another car or truck for nearly an hour. To the south is the Elkhorn Range stretching across the distant horizon. Puffy clouds push over the Wallowa Mountains to the north and I wonder if the road I see leading there is ours. Or, will we skirt west along the valley floor?

I am utterly, perfectly alone. No one is within miles of me save for Rose and Patti. Many uncounted minutes pass until they rise into view, crest the hill, and speed past me, down the other side and into a small valley. The road unwinds like a ribbon from a spool rolling over open spaces, past acres of grazing fields and cattle, hay stacked four bales high and tucked under the protection of a small pole barn, and finally past a town sign by the side of the road, "Pondosa."

We've arrived at the geographic center of the United States. That's what a handmade sign declares in bold black paint.

We lean our bikes against fence posts and walk across a gravel lot to the two-story, wood-framed Pondosa Store. A neon sign inside a front window shines "Open" so we push the door and walk in. The room inside looks more like an old hotel lobby than a store. An older man sits in what appears to be a recliner chair in a room to our left. A television screen is glowing. Is this someone's living room?

Bob Bennett, 98, gets up from his seat and walks over to greet us. Lori Brock, Bob's daughter, appears from a back room. They warmly invite us into the store, the next room straight ahead. I have many questions and both Bob and Lori are happy to answer them all. But before I can start, Bob points to a framed newspaper article hanging on the wall, a copy of the Aug. 18, 2021, issue of the *Baker City Herald*. It's barely a month old, Bob quickly notes. Everything you need to know is right there but go ahead and ask your questions, he says.

The article, written by reporter Lisa Britton, is headlined: "Eastern Oregon town is gone, but its namesake store remains"

Our shoes click across linoleum as Patti, Rose, and I walk inside the small store space. We look for something to enjoy once we sit on a nearby sundeck. Ice cream, savory chips, cold drinks?

"My husband and I try to maintain this nice little oasis for people to stop at during the summer," Lori says. "An occasional neighbor comes in for groceries and an occasional traveler comes by and stops. We've created some camping spots here and some picnic areas, so we work around here trying to keep that up and keep the store open."

This is remote Union County.

"We're kind of self-sufficient out here," she says. "If we lose our power, we've got backup generators and wood stoves."

This once was an active timber town; a mill opened in 1926 bringing workers and families to this area about 25 miles north of Baker City. Life was good, albeit hard. As many as 500 people lived here in its prime. There was a town center consisting of a large boarding house, now the building in which we stand, and a second structure that served as post office, general store, and gas station. Families lived in small, company-owned homes while single men resided at the boarding house.

An old photo circa the 1950s shows more than 20 cars and pickup trucks parked around the post office building and this old, white house. "They had a butcher shop inside the post office and there were a few groceries and whatnot," Lori says. "It also was the offices for the mill with the payroll and everything."

The mill finally closed in 1959. Employees and families began moving away, and the post office's last postmarked mail was dated March 31, 1959.

Two California men, meanwhile, were on a mission of their own making. With Alaska becoming the country's 49th state in January and Hawaii on its way to becoming No. 50, William O. and B. J. Holmes of Research Publications, Inc., took it upon themselves to determine the country's new geographical center. After two misplaced attempts, they determined the center point for all 50 states was at 45 degrees, 8 minutes and 53 seconds north latitude and 117 degrees, 32 minutes and 10 seconds west longitude. That spot is 19 miles northeast of Pondosa deep in the Wallowa-Whitman National Forest.

The Holmeses concluded few would ever go there so they staked their sign instead in Pondosa. By April 7, Pondosa was unofficially declared the geographical center of the United States. But this new-found celebrity status did nothing to save the community. By June 1959, almost all of Pondosa was gone.

"The story goes that there were some guys still working up on the mill site and either someone tossed a cigarette or a spark from welding cutting torches started a fire," Lori says. "That caught some grass on fire and without any way to put it out, the fire just roared through this whole town and any of the buildings or houses that were left burned.

"It caught that store on fire, too," she says, referring to the post office building. "It came up through the grass and everybody was trying to help put it out, but they couldn't save the store."

The boarding house sustained roof damage but the building was saved, and it remains one of the few remaining vestiges of a town long gone.

The property eventually went to auction and was purchased by Lester Gaddy, Lori's uncle. When Lester passed away in 1982. Pondosa went to his sister, Lori's mother, Jean, who with Bob moved from Eugene to live on the property. Jean died in 2015 after an illness. "That left Dad by himself. We were living down in Idaho and he wanted to be here, but this place is too much for one older person to keep up, so we decided we'd move up here with him to help out."

Bob still stays active driving his tractor and four-wheeler to survey his property. He admits to enjoying chatting with customers who stop by. "I'm pretty stable," he volunteers. "I don't have a lot of disabilities, but I do have one and that's my hearing, so people have to forgive me for that."

Lori says the sundeck, set atop the post office building foundation, was built in her mother's memory. "She really wanted a little park here so people could stop and have a cold beverage and a snack. It's a nice, peaceful place with sunshine, trees, and shade."

We say our goodbyes and take our drinks to Jean's deck. A little sun and a little shade. Very peaceful.

We're back on Highway 203, the Mineral Springs Highway, with another 22 miles ahead before we revisit Union. We pedal on as the road slowly ramps up from creek beds and fields toward the tree line. My bike computer reads the elevation at 3,691 feet above sea level as we enter the Wallowa-Whitman National Forest. My legs are weary as we climb. Suddenly, my left knee signals the brain: We have pain. Nothing serious yet, the knee says, but be aware. Pedal stroke. Twinge. Pedal stroke, Twinge. It's the same signal I feel each March as I leave winter hibernation and get back on the bike. The left knee is weak, I say each year. I simply need to get back in shape. By April, the knee is fine.

But I can't recall ever being in such strong riding condition as I am now after a summer in which I steadily rode to the top of the McKenzie Pass twice in June and willed myself over the Shaniko-Fossil Highway near Clarno. I've ridden more than 2,500 miles this year and the same knee that told me to stop running 13 years ago is yapping at me once more. Is it an injury? Is it fatigue? Or is it simply the fact we've just climbed 1,000 feet in seven miles and the old knee has had enough for the day?

Shut up, knee, the brain says. The summit is just around the bend. But is it? I don't know. Keep going.

I stop counting the twinges. Then, as quickly as they started, they stop. And, surprisingly, we've arrived at Catherine Summit. Crisis averted. With a little rest and some cold water from the car's ice cooler, we're back on the road. Now it's time for a 1,000-foot descent to Catherine Creek State Park, a picnic table, and a leisurely lunch.

I remain exhausted after lunch. We pull over in the town of Cove 17 miles and nearly 90 minutes later. The Cove Drive-In across the street sells ice cream and we're all thinking the same thing. Rose and Patti are inside before I can change out of my bike shoes. They return with cones; I eventually buy a cup of vanilla and chocolate ice cream. They finish their cones in short order and prepare to ride. I'm in no hurry now. It's my turn to drive. I lean against the car shaded by a large tree, wave as they depart, and slowly savor my prize.

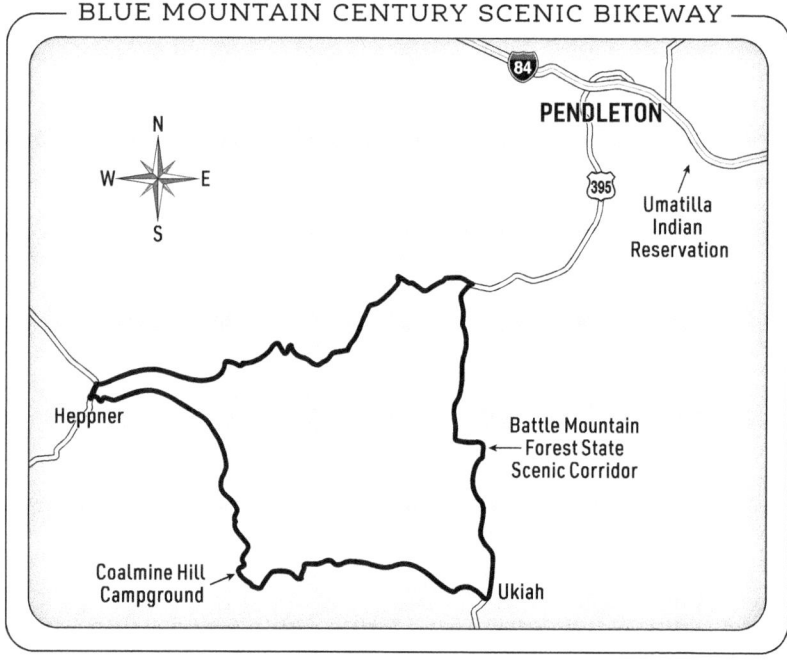

BLUE MOUNTAIN CENTURY SCENIC BIKEWAY

(17)

'This Landscape is Sacred'
Blue Mountain Century Scenic Bikeway

• • •

Start and Finish: Heppner
Distance: 108 miles
Elevation Gain: 8,211 feet
Rating: Extreme

Pendleton – October 2, 2021

Wheat fields yield to ponderosa pines, Douglas firs, spruce and larch trees as Patti and I climb toward the tree line heading south on Highway 395. After 15 miles, we find Rose waiting near the summit of Battle Mountain.

We passed an entrance to the Battle Mountain Forest State Scenic Corridor, a small state picnic area, about a mile back. This is the approximate location of the final battle of the Bannock War, when a coalition of native tribes banded together in an attempt to stop white settlers from taking over these lands. History called this the Bannock War because it was initiated by the Bannock tribe from what is now Idaho. This clash on July 8, 1878, was won by the U.S. cavalry in what is documented as the last uprising by native peoples in the Pacific Northwest.

While the military won the day, this land has been and remains the home of the Cayuse, Walla Walla, and Umatilla people. It was theirs long before white settlers moved in. Today, we pedal along roads that once were horse trails.

The Blue Mountain Century Scenic Bikeway passes 14 miles south of Pendleton, but we detoured to spend last night in town. Pendleton is famous for the annual Pendleton Round-Up rodeo that attracts about 50,000 people every September to "Let 'Er Buck." Pendleton is about three hours east of Portland via Interstate 84, and an hour's drive from La Grande. The city's downtown has a colorful history steeped in cowboy traditions. The Pendleton Woolen Mills, known for its popular blankets and apparel lines, started here as a wool processing facility in 1893.

I'm drawn, however, to the Confederated Tribes of the Umatilla Indian Reservation east of town and the Tamástslikt Cultural Institute where exhibits, timelines, and interactive displays present the history of the Cayuse, Umatilla, and Walla Walla tribes and tell the ongoing story of the tribes' cultures. It also explains the Oregon Trail and western expansion from a different frame of reference. This is the story of a people who have lived here for more than 16,000 years.

Tamástslikt means interpreter in the native Waluulapam dialect, and as director of the cultural institute, Bobbie Conner is well suited to add perspective to the land she calls "the cradle of our existence, the place we belong."

Bobbie looks at the land in a larger sense rather than areas divided by artificial, legislated boundaries because "our presence here is part of a massive continuum and our bond to this landscape is inextricable culturally."

Informed that we had visited the Oregon Trail, she offers a different take on the mass migration.

"The philosophy of our people is not to be stingy or hateful.

The generosity and hospitality in our culture is well known," Bobbie says of her ancestors. "We took care of pitiful travelers and almost everybody who came here early on including the explorers were pretty pitiful. Pioneers' children had no shoes by the time they got here, their horses and livestock were skinny and pitiful by the time they got to the interior Pacific Northwest so there was no reason to consider them a threat. We saw them as pretty helpless."

The immigrants brought two threats with them, Bobbie explains. One was technology. "They had some power with their guns and their metals."

The other was disease in the form of bacteria and viruses for which native peoples had no immunities. The result was sickness, epidemics, and death. "We didn't expect to get their diseases."

Bobbie likes to talk about the land. "It doesn't matter where Lewis and Clark went. It doesn't matter where the Oregon Trail ruts are," she says. "What matters is that our ancestors are buried all over this landscape. It's not just where the museum is or just the Umatilla reservation, it's this vast landscape where I feel like a neophyte because I don't know the canyons and gullies and swales and saddles and creeks where my uncles hunted for generations and generations and generations."

There's a place near Union where Bobbie goes, a spot her grandmother enjoyed camping as a child. It's Catherine Creek. "I feel like she's present there because this is one of her favorite places at the turn of the last century, 122 years ago, where she slept as a little girl."

I'm transported. We stopped at Catherine Creek State Park for lunch. We watched the creek's rushing waters as Bobbie's grandmother most likely did.

"Almost every freeway and highway and railroad track follows some trail that was here before. From my perspective, every road in our homeland has its origins in the trails of our ancestors," Bobbie says. "This landscape is sacred, and it's not just the surface. It's the aquifer, it's the terrain, it's all of the elevation changes. It's all sacred and I think the importance for cyclists is two-fold. One, you're traveling the landscape more like our ancestors did than any other traveler today, right? You're on a bike and closer to the land.

"And two, you're taking the time to engage and be in that land. It's a sense of mindfulness and conscientious traveling."

The Blue Mountain Century Scenic Bikeway, one of the most challenging of Oregon's 17 scenic routes, officially starts and ends in Heppner slightly more than 60 miles southwest of Pendleton. But we devised our own plan, starting south of town where Highways 395 and 72 meet. We'll ride clockwise, spend tonight in Heppner, and complete the loop tomorrow.

There's some significant climbing today, about 5,400 feet over 71 miles. Patti and I completed more than a third of that work on our way up Battle Mountain. Now Rose gets to glide 10 miles downhill thanks to our driver/rider rotation. Long downhills like this are unusual. We're coasting along a fairly straight road with grades averaging 3 to 4 percent much of the way.

With no traffic and no worries, my mind wanders. What a peaceful morning, I think, looking east across the plain. What did we have for dinner last night? Where are we eating tonight? Where is Patti going to meet us for the next shuttle exchange? Is that the town of Ukiah in the distance? Am I still going downhill? How long have we been doing this?

We rotate our pedals from time to time, not to gain speed but to simply keep our legs moving. I look down and see spider silk stretching across my handlebar. It appears I've picked up a passenger, an unknown spider species "ballooning" or traveling in the morning breeze. I swipe the silk away with my right hand, shake it free, and regrip the bar. Moments later, I see more silk has landed. This sequence repeats several times as we pass acre after acre of wheat.

And still, Rose and I continue downhill.

Sadly, it finally ends. We turn onto a forest road and stop by the waiting car. Patti has her bike positioned and is ready to start even though she knows it's time to go uphill again. She and Rose begin while I drive up this narrow blacktop, Forest Road 53, known locally as the Western Route Road, across the Umatilla National Forest. The landscape is open to the north and forested to the south, and in a few weeks the road may be blocked by snow and accessible only by snowmobile. But it's ours today.

We pass a turn to the Aspen Grove Interpretative Site, a U.S. Forest Service outpost focusing on conservation and aspen forest management. The road is lined on both sides by aspens with green-turning-yellow-turning-gold leaves fluttering in an afternoon breeze as if to wave as we go by. The nearly round leaves make clicking, applauding sounds in the wind.

The trees grow thicker as we elevate. The deciduous larches show their gold needles on this October afternoon, contrasting against the green of the nearby evergreens. I enjoy the sense of escape whenever I ride into a forest but today seems different, perhaps better. I've never been on this road before and possibly never will be again. This is a once-in-a-lifetime moment, a discovery all its own. Perhaps Bobbie Conner's ancestors followed this trail.

We pass an entrance to Coalmine Hill Campground, U.S. Forest Service land, and bend north toward Heppner along Willow Creek Road. There are 30 more miles, almost all downhill, before we get to town. It's agreed; we divide the day's final miles in three parts so everyone can enjoy this descent. Especially Patti.

Heppner – October 3, 2021

We gather at a sidewalk table in front of the Northwestern Motel for a breakfast of coffee, muffins, bananas, and anything else we have in the cooler. This is our low-budget yet cozy, comfortable overnight stop in downtown Heppner. It's chilly at an elevation of 2,192 feet at 8 a.m. in early October. We position and reposition our chairs to capture any warmth from the rising sun. A man, perhaps in his 50s, slows to say good morning as he walks his dog. A group of hunters we met last evening is already gone. They probably left hours ago.

We, too, will soon be on our way. We need only follow Highway 74 back to yesterday's starting junction and we will have completed another bikeway. The streets are quiet, void of traffic this Sunday morning as we ride along Main Street and turn east. Ahead of us is the Morrow County Courthouse, dominant from its perch atop a rise at the end of East May Street. A long, stone staircase leads from the sidewalk to the front doors of this bluestone edifice. A clock tower adds to its grand presence.

The original courthouse, built shortly after Heppner became the Morrow County seat in 1885, was erected on the same small hill about 200 yards from Main Street. Historians surmise local residents sought higher ground for the building after a flood two years earlier wiped out much of the town. That structure was torn down in 1902 and this courthouse was constructed in its place. It's remained the center of county justice ever since.

We stop for pictures and then pedal out of town for a tranquil ride to finish our loop. We follow the two-lane Highway 74 between small hills as it snakes its way to our destination. After about 20 miles, Rose and I see the car parked on the opposite side of the road. Patti emerges waving caution and pointing out road debris. A dead animal, slightly larger than a basketball, is in the middle of our lane but I'm unsure what it is; I've never seen anything like it. Thin, white sticks about three inches long are scattered across the road.

"Porcupine quills," Patti says with authority. "Don't run over them."

Porcupines have about 30,000 quills, all lightly attached to the skin. From its appearance, it appears this poor rodent lost much of its defense system when it was struck by a vehicle. I later learn that each quill is about 2 to 3 inches long and has 700 to 800 barbs that make extraction from a predator's flesh difficult and painful. I don't want to find out what a quill can do to a bike tire, so I dismount and carry the bike across the quill field.

As we cross, a young man driving a pickup truck arrives. Using a tool, perhaps an axe, he pushes the porcupine, rolling it off the road. We thank him and he casually waves as though this is a common occurrence. We go in different directions, he toward Heppner and we toward the end of another scenic bikeway.

SHERAR'S FALLS SCENIC BIKEWAY

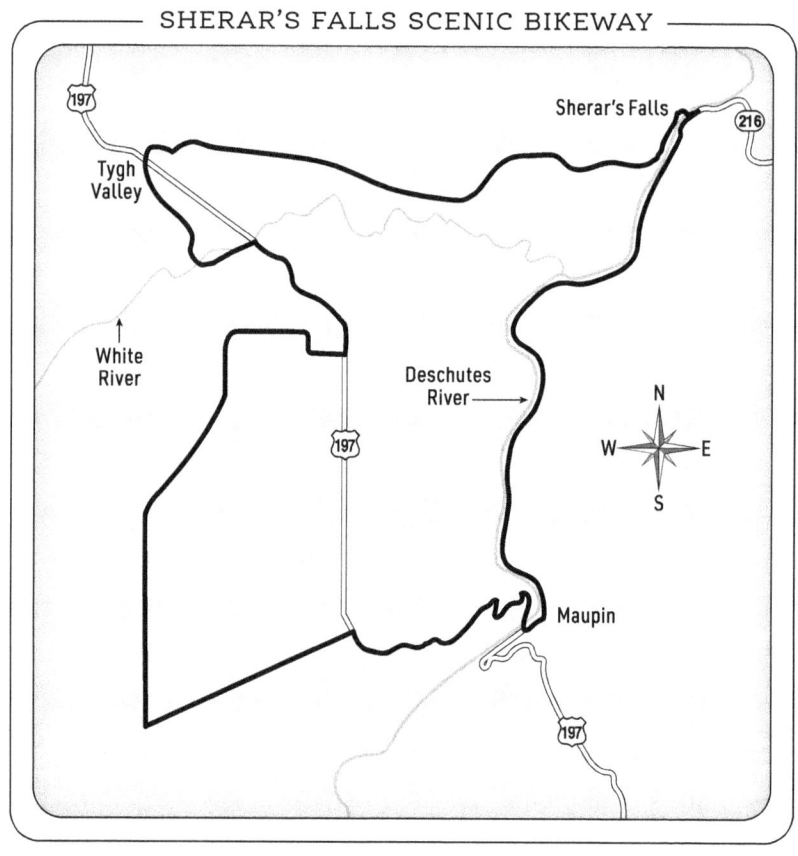

Clockwise? Counterclockwise?

Sherar's Falls Scenic Bikeway

• • •

Start and Finish: Maupin
Distance: 33 miles
Elevation Gain: 1,727 feet
Rating: Moderate

Maupin – October 4, 2021

Anyone following Highway 197 from Central Oregon to The Dalles has driven through Maupin. The road drops down from the high desert plateau, revealing the town nestled in the canyon below against a bend of the Deschutes River. Once across a short bridge, the road rises into the city center and exits to destinations north. I've driven through Maupin many times, but never stopped until now.

The air is cold at 8 a.m. as we emerge this morning from our Imperial River Co. hotel rooms and roll our bikes to a riverside patio where we enjoyed dinner the night before. Waiting for our autumn day to warm up, we delay our departure and take time to review the ride map. The Sherar's Falls route is a one-day loop, starting and ending at the hotel. Riders can choose to go uphill into the commercial district, but the elevation profile is discouraging. More than 1,000 of the day's 1,732 feet of climbing would occur in the first six-plus miles if we go this way.

Doug Parrow, one of the state scenic bikeways committee's route evaluators, emailed me last night suggesting we consider riding counterclockwise to avoid the steep problem. "Sherar's Falls is signed in both directions. I actually prefer counterclockwise," he wrote.

Susie Miles, on the other hand, suggests first-timers go the other way. "I would certainly do it clockwise which means I would go up through town," she says. "It makes more sense to go slow up through town rather than being on your brakes the whole time as you are coming down through town on your descent."

Susie is well-positioned to know. She and husband Rob own and operate the 25-room Imperial River Co. hotel where many visiting cyclists stay. She was the community proponent when this bikeway was under state consideration, but she doesn't take credit for the route's inclusion. It was Alex Phillips' idea.

"Give Alex credit," Susie says of the original state bikeways coordinator who concluded Maupin and Wasco County have one of the best natural bike routes in the state. "She said Maupin is an area that is often forgotten about because we're not Bend, we're not Central Oregon, and we're not the Columbia Gorge. We're not Mount Hood or Eastern Oregon yet we're super accessible. She thought it would be a pretty easy bikeway to get pushed through [the approval process] and I thought that she was probably right," Susie says.

Sherar's Falls was designated a scenic bikeway in 2017, and now cyclists drive from throughout the state to enjoy these open roads whether they ride clockwise or counterclockwise.

After weighing our options, we go with Doug's suggestion and start out easy. Counterclockwise. The first eight miles are pancake flat along the Deschutes River toward the namesake falls. We feel lucky to share this peaceful road with only a few fluttering birds on a cloudy yet so far dry day. It's an encouraging start after a discouraging weather forecast.

This Bureau of Land Management access road ends and we turn left over Sherar's Bridge. There's nothing at the turn except four parked cars and trucks and a few men fishing nearby. Some stand on platforms exclusively used by native peoples—wooden scaffolds with decks extending horizontally from the shoreline. Some use large hooped dipnets attached to poles to catch the salmon or steelhead below. We watch from the road.

Settlers began altering this landscape in 1860 when John Y. Todd built a bridge across the river and then replaced it in 1862 when the first span washed away. Joseph Sherar eventually bought the bridge, attached his name to it, and with his wife Jane invested in a new business enterprise. He improved the road and instituted a crossing toll. He also built a stagecoach station with a three-story Sherar Bridge Hotel, livery, and shops. Sherar died in 1908, the historical society's Oregon History Project explains, and the arrival of the railroad in the river canyon eventually diverted customers. Other owners maintained the hotel until it was destroyed by fire in 1940.

There's hardly a trace remaining of those hotel days but two things remain: Sherar's name is still attached to the bridge and nearby waterfalls, and the traditional fishing platforms are still in use just as they were long before the Sherar's arrival.

Highway 216 leads us away from the river, up a hill, out of the canyon, and across open cattle grazing land. Mount Hood appears in the distance, snow-capped above its eastern slopes. We cross Highway 197 and ride into Tygh Valley, a community of a mere 123 people. Molly B's Diner is closed so we pull energy food from our back pockets and find places to sit in an adjacent grassy space. The town is eerily quiet. One car briefly stops at a small store a half block up the street, a passenger goes inside, swiftly returns, and the car is gone.

It's so quiet.

We've reached the halfway point on today's ride, but we need to pick up our pace. The day's weather forecast is beginning to ring true. Clouds are forming in the distance. We head south on Juniper Flat Road, then east on Wapinitia Highway. The road shoulder is wide, a reassuring discovery as large trucks and pickups roar past. And then there's another morale boost. We're rolling downhill. The final six-mile descent has begun. It's not a steep gradient, just enough to assist our pedaling as we continue to gain speed.

We make a right turn and Highway 197 takes us all the way into Maupin. The slope increases as the first gentle raindrops fall, my jacket sleeves flap louder and louder as I descend. The highway curls and enters the main part of town; no time to slow and look around with dark clouds overhead. We drop down the last hill and cross the Deschutes River one more time.

Clockwise? Counterclockwise? We need to come back another day and try it Susie's way.

I also want to spend more time exploring Maupin. Susie says it's worth another trip and I believe her. After all, she and others here have invested their lives and money to make it a destination. That wasn't always the case. This has long been an agricultural area. Susie's family, in fact, has been in the cattle, sheep, and wheat business for decades. She grew up here and admits she couldn't wait to leave after high school. But she and Rob returned, bought a hotel, raised a family, and made a commitment to the Wasco County community.

"I was 17 when I left in the early '90s. Maupin has changed a lot from when I grew up here," she says. "Farms have gotten larger and larger and larger and all the little guys can't afford to farm anymore because they can't make a living, so the number of people working in agriculture has shrunk like you wouldn't even believe. We've seen agriculture die in the late '80s and early '90s."

She returned more than a decade later to rediscover her hometown. Recreation tourism—cycling, rafting, fishing, hunting—had replaced agriculture. The Deschutes River had become an economic engine. Expanded internet bandwidth helped, too.

"Maupin has completely reinvented itself. Some significant things have happened in the last 20 years here like getting fiber internet," Susie says. "Now more people are seeking to live in rural areas. The overall feel has changed so certainly I think differently about it than I did when I was 17."

One final left-hand turn leads us back to Susie's hotel parking lot. We dismount and pose for celebratory pictures, then rack our bikes, and drive home.

Sixteen bikeways in one year is something to remember, but we know there's an asterisk on this accomplishment. Our 17th and final challenge is closed, off limits after deadly wildfires swept through that area a year ago.

We can't go there. Not yet. So, we wait.

(19)

'I Drove Through That Fire'
Cascading Rivers Scenic Bikeway

• • •

Start and Finish: Estacada or Detroit
Distance: 71 miles
Elevation Gain: 4,445 feet from Estacada,
3,300 feet from Detroit
Rating: Challenging

Salem – May 4, 2023

Kevin Cameron leans back in his chair and considers the question: Can you talk with me about the fire?

"Yeah, I'll tell you about it," he says after a beat. "It's easier to talk about it today."

It's been 968 days since a conflagration of wildfires swooped down on the lakefront town of Detroit and the Santiam Valley. Kevin lives in Detroit. He was there the night his community burned to the ground.

"I drove through that fire."

Kevin shares his recollections about the catastrophe that devastated the Marion County communities of Detroit, Gates, and Mill City on September 7-8, 2020. He recounts in detail his movements, the aftermath, and ongoing recovery nearly three years later. Kevin is both a fire survivor and a Marion County

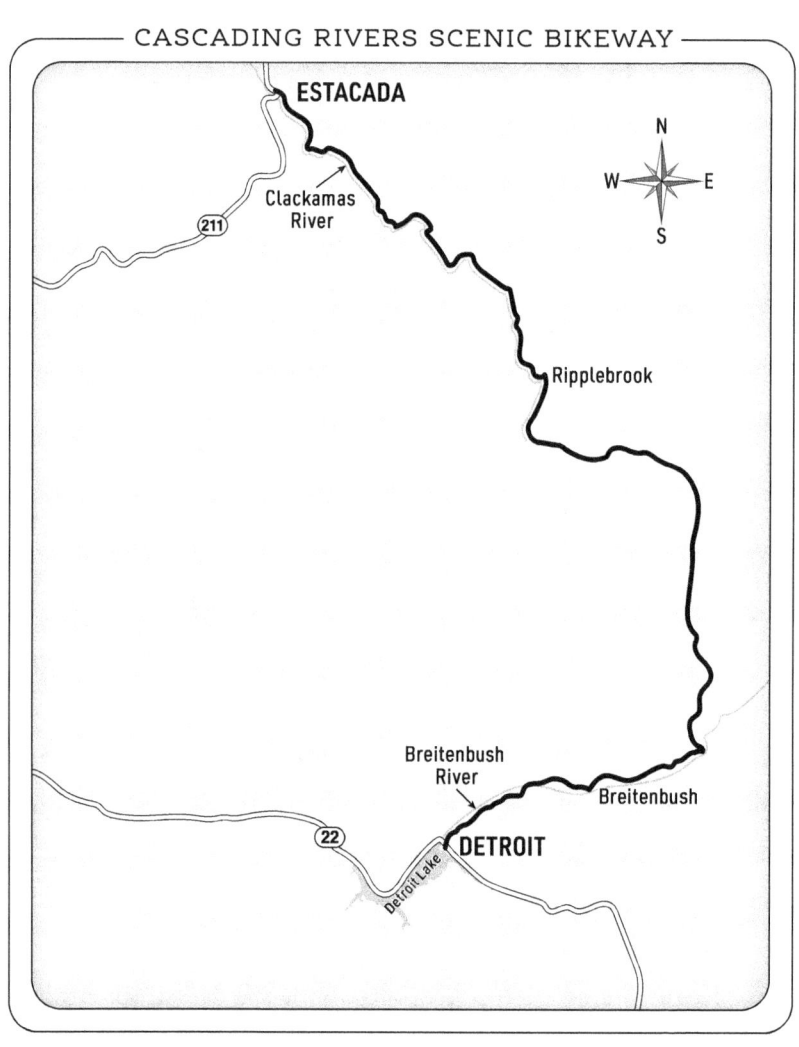

CASCADING RIVERS SCENIC BIKEWAY

ESTACADA

211

Clackamas
River

Ripplebrook

Breitenbush
River

Breitenbush

22

DETROIT

Detroit Lake

N
W   E
S

commissioner, and he shifts roles as he tells his story. He's a Detroit resident and he's a public official. He's a man whose home was inexplicably spared and a friend who strives to help neighbors who lost everything.

"I emotionally toggle."

The 2020 inferno burned to the ground approximately 90 percent of all Detroit buildings that Labor Day weekend, Kevin says. It scarred Mill City and devastated Gates, two communities farther down the Santiam Canyon. Officials had named one fire Lionshead and another Beachie Creek. A third was called Santiam.

Zach Urness, a veteran outdoors writer with the *Statesman Journal* in Salem, saw it coming days before. "I remember that weekend really well because I was up in Detroit," he says. While on a hike, "I climbed Potato Butte, looked out and there was Lionshead. It was just starting to grow."

From the top of Potato Butte northwest of Detroit, Zach could see smoke to the east as it kindled in the wilderness. Zach is well versed on wildfires, their behaviors, and the devastation they cause, and he didn't like what he saw.

"I could see the pyrocumulus clouds rising and rising," he remembers. "I knew that an east wind event was coming and I knew we were in trouble."

The Beachie Creek fire, which started three weeks earlier, would consume homes and timber from Opal Creek to the Santiam Canyon. Meanwhile, the Riverside fire to the north near Estacada was inflicting its own wrath. Beachie Creek and Lionshead, officials later concluded, were ignited by downed power lines. Riverside was human-caused.

The winds pushed smoke from the growing Lionshead fire west over Detroit and the adjacent lake, a popular fishing and boating destination, creating an ominous shadow on Labor Day, Monday, Sept. 7. High winds and heavy smoke left Kevin with a sense of foreboding. "I never did sleep that night because the winds were howling so bad. I could hear the limbs hitting my house. It just wasn't right."

By midnight, residents in communities throughout the canyon were issued "Go Now" orders to evacuate. But this was a difficult task. Fires were raging, tree branches were falling, and smoke obscured visibility on Highway 22, the only major road in or out of the area. Kevin and his weekend houseguests still hurried to his pickup truck and fled.

"It was almost one in the morning and we were dodging stuff on the road and embers were flying," Kevin recounts. "You could see the fire coming over the hill toward the Breitenbush River. We eventually got to Gates and there was fire, but it still wasn't encroaching on the road."

Their escape slowed to a stop in Mill City three miles later. Suddenly and without explanation, Kevin says, "an ODOT truck took off. These guys didn't say anything to me, but I assumed I was supposed to follow. He was going so fast he was pulling fire in and he was pulling the smoke in behind him. I could barely see. My truck was hot. It was like following in fog, so I had to follow the centerline of the road."

A U.S. Forest Service after-event report succinctly summed it up: "The fire caught everyone by surprise."

The Beachie Creek blaze converged with a smaller Santiam fire and then merged with Lionshead at Detroit. Buildings in other communities along the highway, Idanha and Mehama, also were destroyed or heavily damaged. The Beachie Creek/ Santiam claimed 522 buildings including 486 homes, many of which were in Gates. Lionshead took another 278 buildings, 264 of which were homes, primarily in Detroit. The Riverside fire incinerated 277 buildings, including 62 homes.

Kevin Cameron and his guests escaped unharmed. They were lucky. Five people lost their lives. Families lost their homes. People lost their livelihoods.

We safely watched from Salem 55 miles away as smoke invaded the Willamette Valley, blocking the sun and casting a burnt red pall across the sky. Our primary source of information was Zach's online reporting.

By the summer of 2021, almost a year after the fires, the Cascading Rivers Scenic Bikeway remained closed while the National Forest Service and reclamation crews cleared fallen trees, secured hillsides, and made the roads safe for passage. Our bike final ride was on hold.

Estacada – June 28, 2023

The road from Estacada to Detroit fully reopened yesterday for the first time. We're back on our bikes this morning prepared to finish what we set out to do more than two years ago. Today we follow the Clackamas River south from Estacada to Detroit. We pass across acreage scorched by the Riverside fire, climb to the summit of this 71-mile route, and then descend through Lionshead fire country along the Breitenbush River to Detroit.

A 25-mile stretch of the bikeway, Estacada south to Ripplebrook on Highway 224, opened last summer so Patti Rogers, Bob Cortright, Eric Jacobson, and I took advantage and set out for the Mt. Hood National Forest. We rode past North Fork Reservoir and up a gradual, manageable grind through the Clackamas River canyon. We crossed the Carter and Armstrong bridges, passing between their steel trusses as the river ran below us.

There was activity along the way. Traffic stopped several times so crews could perform post-fire recovery work to prevent rockslides down steep slopes alongside the highway. Retaining walls were being installed in some places to catch falling rocks. We could see workers suspended high along the canyon walls in other spots, using hand tools to force suspect rocks down in this controlled setting.

The road surface itself was pockmarked. At first, I thought heavy equipment had damaged the asphalt during cleanup, but a road worker explained each of the countless scars was caused by fallen rocks. The fire also altered our perspective of the steep hillsides. With no tree branches to obscure our view, we could see the chiseled basalt formations extending down like fat fingers to the canyon floor. Before the fire, these fingers were hidden behind a visual blanket of Douglas firs.

We arrived at Ripplebrook Store, snacked, and then retraced our path back to Estacada.

Now Patti, Bob, and I are back in 2023 ready to finish this bikeway. The Ripplebrook Store, a longtime wilderness outpost with supplies, food, maps, and information for campers, bikers, and backpackers, remains closed. The store survived the Riverside fire, but the concessionaire decided to renovate the building while the forest rejuvenates. A Forest Service office only feet away, however, burned down. Such is the random nature of fire.

We push past the store and pick up National Forest Road 46. The wilderness is still. I hear nothing but Patti's bike rolling over the rarely used blacktop as it cuts a swath through standing, healthy, green timber. No chirping birds. No rustling wind. The river eventually reappears with water rushing over rocks breaking the natural silence.

The Clackamas River remains alongside for approximately 15 miles, disappearing behind the trees and reemerging again and again. Scenic bikeways exist to lead cyclists to new destinations. For me, these few miles epitomize the idyllic natural beauty a scenic bikeway reveals deep in the wilderness. My pedaling slows. Perhaps I don't want this to end.

In time, an orange, temporary sign declares "ROAD CLOSED AHEAD." We're 18 miles from Detroit and we keep going, knowing the road opened yesterday and the sign likely only needs to be retrieved. We leave the thick trees about a quarter mile later for total devastation, from lush forest to a post-apocalyptic desolation. Countless stark, blackened tree trunks somberly stand on both sides of the road. Hundreds of large, long, salvage logs are horizontally stacked awaiting collection. Rocks and charred wood are scattered among tree stumps. I try to envision the inferno that raged across this land but I have no point of reference. I hope I never know.

This scenario repeats itself as we roll down toward Detroit Lake. Sections of standing forest spared during the fire alternate with scarred acreage. Smooth road asphalt becomes rutted and gouged by emergency equipment and falling objects. We pass the entrance to Breitenbush Hot Springs, a popular retreat since the late 1970s that sustained enormous losses during the fires when 75 buildings were destroyed. And, we stop along the Breitenbush River to study the hillside on the other side of the water, trying to picture how the winds pushed flames through the canyon.

Kevin Cameron returned less than 48 hours after fire swept through town.

"We got to Detroit and I looked to the left and the gas station was gone. It was just smoking," he remembers. "The store was still there but everything on the other side of Main Street was gone except the post office. There was a fire engine burned in the street. We went around a corner and there were propane tanks still squirting out fire. I've never been in a war zone. Bless those that have, but I thought we'd just been bombed. Trailers across the street were melted and smoking. It was pretty weird.

"I went down my street and the first two houses were burnt and smoking, and the shed at the next house was gone and the house was kind of blistered from the fire," he says.

Through it all, the Cameron home was still standing.

As a Marion County commissioner, Kevin had work to do. The survivors were his friends and neighbors; they also were his constituents. People needed water, for example, because the city water system was destroyed.

"I had some survivor's guilt," he says. "I asked myself 'Why? Why is my house still standing when 90 percent of the structures are gone?' I turned that around and said, well, I'm here for a purpose."

Kevin joined the city planning commission and the Detroit Lake Foundation board of directors so he could help rebuild. Together, the community raised money. The old high school, which survived the fire, was converted into a community center. The state provided tax relief for those affected by the fires. Detroit slowly began to bounce back.

"So, now I'm watching these homes being built and it's really neat to see the city come back."

Fires that Monday and Tuesday devastated Oregon, burning about 1,500 square miles from the Warm Springs Reservation in Central Oregon to Lincoln City on the coast. Intense winds pushed another deadly fire, termed the Almeda Fire, across about 3,000 acres in two days along Southern Oregon's Interstate 5 corridor. Homes were destroyed. Three more people died.

Some of the fires were started by lightning strikes days, even weeks before Labor Day. At least two fires were sparked by downed electrical power lines. The cause of the Almeda Fire remains under investigation more than three years later though officials say it was likely caused by a person. High winds fanned every blaze.

Zach Urness reported in an August 25, 2021, *Statesman Journal* article: "The fires made more Oregonians, particularly on the verdant west side of the Cascades, far more aware of the dangers of wildfire. Oregon always has had a wildfire season, but the flames typically stayed in the mountains or forested areas, rarely threatening or burning into urban corridors. That all changed last Labor Day."

We complete our final three miles looking down to the Breitenbush River and eventually the northernmost finger of Detroit Lake. The contrast is distinct. The lake, nearly full with winter rainwater and snowmelt, attracts people looking to boat and fish yet the nearby hillsides still show the scars of fire. We cross Highway 22 into town and discover empty property lots where homes and businesses once stood. In other spaces, new homes have been built. Food trucks are positioned to fill a void created when the popular Cedars Restaurant burned to the ground. We can hear power saws cutting wood and hammers pounding nails. The community is slowly bouncing back.

We rack our bikes for the final time on this adventure and walk a half block to a Mexican food truck. Sitting at a picnic table with our lunches, conversation turns as it often does with Bob's question:

"Where do we go next?"

Epilogue

"Where do we go next?"

Good question. Change is afoot; there soon may be new roads to explore.

Cycle Oregon is working with the state Parks and Recreation Department to try to revitalize the scenic bikeways program. The nonprofit organization has signed on to reformat a dormant advisory committee and manage program operations. It is developing a new plan for consideration and approval that may take the scenic bikeways concept in a new and more inclusive direction.

"This program has done a lot for Oregon, but it needs to adapt and it needs to evolve," says Steve Schulz, Cycle Oregon's executive director. "If you're only going to focus on paved roads, that's not going to be accessible to everybody that wants to ride bikes. These [existing bikeways] are not beginner routes and if we want to say, 'hey anybody can ride in Oregon,' they're not gonna be able to ride these."

To that end, Steve says, a new approach is being drafted that may include gravel roads, mountain bike trails, even non-motorized pathways.

"It's great now, but it could be better and it needs to be better," he says. "It needs to adapt with where we are now. We need more accessible routes. We need different distances. We need better community development. We need different surfaces. We need to showcase Oregon in different ways and make it accessible to more people. We want to build a bigger, more impactful program that really incorporates celebrating the state and the culture and the communities and history and not just 100 miles of really great road to ride on."

Here are a few more updates.

Like many hospitality businesses, The Crazy Norwegian in Port Orford struggled during the COVID pandemic. Dianne Hosford turned to takeout ordering when her restaurant customers couldn't come inside. She added a patio, too. "The locals avoid us in the summer," she says. Business is "80-20 travelers in the summer and 60-40 locals in the winter.

"I get a ton of bikers, too. I got a bike rack in 2023."

Bike Indy Oregon is working.

"I see success when I walk downtown," says Shawn Irvine, economic development director for the city of Independence. "On any nice day, and on many not-so-nice days, there is a collection of bikes in front of Ovenbird [bakery] and BREW [coffee shop] and more rolling through town. I see lots of cars parked in Riverview Park or at City Hall with bike racks on the back—people who are out for a day ride and may stick around for dinner or a beer. Most importantly, our storefronts are full."

Available data indicates downtown visitation is up 66 percent from 2017 to 2022, 14 percent alone since 2019 despite COVID, he says.

About 4,000 people attended Brownsville's annual Stand By Me Day on July 23, 2023. "We weren't sure what to expect this year because it fell on a Sunday, but as usual, people came from across the country and around the world," Linda McCormick says. "We held our event on the street in front of the Linn County Historical Museum and closed off the street to traffic."

The traditional blueberry pie eating contest took place and "four local friends dressed up just like the four boys in the movie and walked around town. They were a hit. All the fans seemed to want a photo with them."

Richard Meyers retired in October 2023 after serving in local government for 36 years, 26 of those as Cottage Grove's city manager. He's now spending more time with his wife, children, and 10 grandchildren. He's camping, kayaking, and restoring his 130-year-old house.

And, he has more time to ride his bike. "I am looking forward to the opportunities," he says. "I will be riding the Covered Bridges Scenic Bikeway regularly."

Lori Brock reports from Pondosa that her father Bob Bennett celebrated his 100th birthday in June 2023. "Dad is really doing well," Lori says. "He's still waiting on customers in the store every day. He really enjoys that."

The National Oregon Trail Interpretive Center in Baker City is scheduled to reopen in late May 2024 after extensive construction, field manager Sarah Sherman says. "The galleries will look the same upon reopening, but we have plans for upgrades in the future."

A new, $5 million Kam Wah Chung Interpretive Center in John Day, meanwhile, is on track for a Spring 2026 opening. The facility will be three times the size of the existing space, site curator Don Merritt says, and will include exhibit space, a theater, virtual reality room, conference room, gift shop, and collections storage that Don says will meet federal curation facility standards.

More than 1,000 riders stayed overnight in 2023 at the Spoke'n Hostel in Mitchell, Jalet Farrell says. That number should grow when camping space is added in 2024 for self-supported cyclists.

Meanwhile, local community support for visiting cyclists expanded late in 2023. The Wheeler County Trading Co., the town's grocery, hardware, lumber, and feed store, added showers for touring riders and a laundromat.

Jalet also shares a new story. "One couple who stayed with

us later hiked the Italian Alps and some of the surrounding countries," she says. "In Switzerland, they heard another couple speaking English and struck up a conversation. It was discovered both couples had stayed with us as guests."

Our group continued to explore by bicycle in 2023, expanding our reach as far south as San Diego and north to Victoria, British Columbia. And, like our scenic bikeway rides, we made many personal discoveries along the way. We found them in forests as Natalie Inoyue predicted we would. We also found them in the spacious open spaces Alex Phillips loves.

I've long maintained that travel is much more than seeing famous landmarks in distant lands. Each trip should include conversations with locals even when we as visitors speak the foreign language. Understanding, or at least attempting to understand, others is a step toward bridging gaps and appreciating cultures. We should turn left when other tourists turn right. When we do, we're rarely disappointed.

These 17 scenic bikeways became a long series of left turns. While language was never a problem, we met people of different Oregon cultures and different political beliefs. And, there was one common theme: We were interested in their communities and they were happy to talk with us about it.

"I enjoy revisiting places around the state where I'd been many years ago. I'm always curious to see each one, thinking about why people settled there and what their lifestyle is like," Patti says. "I gained more appreciation for the differences. 'I'm from Oregon' could mean I'm a Portland hipster or a rancher far from any city or a small-town storekeeper trying to stay in business since the mill or cannery closed. I find that people usually like to talk if you ask them about their hometown."

And, there's an appreciation of the land.

"It really sinks in during these rides how the scale of the landscape is different by bike," Patti continues. "The scenery's details are different from what's seen from a car, or while walking. The terrain is always a factor. A long or steep hill is very evident by bike. It requires patience and determination. Reaching the summit is cause for celebration, or relief, and the well-earned descent can bring childlike joy."

Bob is reminded of a quick exchange he once had with Jennifer Donnelly while we were riding her favorite backroads in the Hood River Valley. "It was a sunny spring day and I was suddenly struck by the incredible scenery and landscape, verdant orchards, quiet winding roads, deep forests, long views to Mount Adams, Mount Hood and the Columbia River she got to experience almost every day. I said to her 'You know, you live in a really beautiful place.' She smiled that beautiful smile of hers back at me and replied 'I know.'

"When we ride the backroads around Oregon, that's what we get to experience, the incredible depth and beauty of the place, the landscape where we live," Bob says. "Cycling immerses us in that landscape, makes us a part of that landscape in a unique and powerful way."

This is why we travel; this is why we ride. We enjoy the adventure, the physical test, and the camaraderie. We want to explore outside our comfort zone in places we've never seen and moments we've never experienced. With a wider lens, we see it's also for a sense of place, an appreciation for the land, the people who live here now, and the centuries of people who walked here before us.

Acknowledgments

A group of cyclists riding together is called a peloton. I'm fortunate to have had a peloton of riders, editors, family, and friends who have helped me get this book to the finish line.

I thank first, and most importantly, my wife Carla Shryock for her steadfast support from the moment I first suggested writing a book. She's been my editor, business manager, marketing and sales consultant, social media manager, and my moral support. Then there are the riders on the road: Carla, Sam Shryock, Patti Rogers, Bob Cortright, Eric Jacobson, Elise Hendrickson, Rose Owens, Mischa O'Reilly, and Robert Mansolillo. They all made the road more enjoyable.

Thanks also are extended to Bronte Dod, who edited and improved my words, and Dave Caplan, who created the maps, designed the cover, formatted the pages, and made sure this book looked great.

A special thanks to Sheila Alfsen and Carrie Gordon. Sheila

served as my geology teacher and advisor; Carrie filled in the gaps when it came to Crooked River and thunder eggs. Linda McCormick told me all I needed to know about Brownsville and Stand By Me Days and then helped research the histories of Ira and Julia Henderson. Zach Urness guided me through the 2020 wildfires.

And, to all the family and friends who kept asking about this project for nearly three years, thank you for nudging me along. Your interest helped keep me pedaling forward.